ADJAI

The African slave boy who became a Bishop

A personal Mémoir

by

D1418729

ARNOLD AWOONOR-GORDON

HIS GREAT-GREAT-GRANDSON

EDITED BY WINSTON FORDE

www.songlome.com

Cover adapted by Khadi Mansaray

THE LATE BISHOP SAMUEL ADJAI
CROWTHER
R.I.P

PREFACE

I was spurred on to write the life of my Great-great-grandfather, the late Bishop Samuel Adjai Crowther, when I read an article in a local British newspaper that '**a service of Thanksgiving and repentance**' had been held in Canterbury Cathedral in Kent to mark the 150 years of the consecration of Bishop Samuel Adjai Crowther. I was surprised that such a service could have been held without any of the many direct descendants living in Kent, London and the South East of England, a few miles from where the ceremony had taken place, being present. Because I had previously written to the Librarian of the Cathedral to ask whether there were any records in the archives about one of the most momentous events in the history of the Anglican Church, mindful that 2014 would be one hundred and fifty years since he became the first black bishop and had been informed that they held no such records in their archives.

So, we the descendants of our illustrious ancestor were deeply disappointed that when the arrangements for the service to take place on 30th June, 2014 were being made, no one had taken the trouble to find out whether any of his descendants were alive who should have been invited to attend the ceremony. In his sermon at the service, Archbishop Welby spoke about the racism that Bishop Crowther faced from within and outside the Anglican Church when he was made bishop, and apologised on behalf of the church. But I cannot help but wonder whether the racism he spoke about, does not still exist within the Anglican community one hundred and fifty years later. When the descendants of the bishop who live just a stone's throw from the place where the ceremony would take place, had been completely ignored.

So, I have taken upon myself the task of writing a personal memoire to show that Bishop Samuel Adjai Crowther, the slave boy who became a bishop, and the patriarch of my family, left a lasting legacy, which we have inherited. His descendants are living today, not only in the United Kingdom and the United States of America, but also in the Gambia, Sierra Leone, Ghana and Nigeria and are still alive as shown on the family tree at page 216.

I have used his African name of Adjai throughout, which is usually given to a baby born with the umbilical cord round his neck, according to Nigerian custom. I was assured by my grandmother, one of several grandchildren of the Bishop, and one who knew him well, that he preferred to be called by his African name of which he was justifiably proud. He became known to his many grandchildren as Grandpa Adjai, and his wife answered proudly to Grandma Asano.

My Grandmother, Emilie Brigas Williams, was one of the thirteen children of Susan and the eldest of the three daughters of Adjai and Asano. She married the Rev. George Pompey Nicol, Chaplain to the Forces in the Gambia. She promptly adopted their combined surnames and henceforth was known as Susan Crowther-Nicol. My grandmother, with whom I lived as a boy and young man, is my direct link with the Bishop, as she knew him as well as I knew my grandmother.   So, I can boast with all conviction that I knew someone who knew Samuel Adjai Crowther, the first, and for many years, the only black bishop, and that I heard many stories about him directly from his granddaughter.

So, in order to effectively commemorate his memory, I have used Adjai throughout the book, and his other name of Samuel only now and again. I am sad that I did not meet him, as he died some forty years before I was born. However, I clearly remember meeting his son Archdeacon Dandeson Crowther, when as a young boy of about five I was taken by my grandmother to visit her uncle Dan at his house on Pademba Road, opposite Wellington Street in Freetown. He was a very old man then, and I remember being frightened to meet someone so old. He was sitting in a chair wrapped in a shawl and wearing purple slippers. I remember the slippers distinctly as I had never seen that colour before. When my grandmother pushed me towards him to sit on his lap, I cringed and hid behind her skirt, so frightening did he look. I wish I had not done so and gone and sat on his lap, so that today I could boast that I had sat on the lap of the son of the great bishop. But, I was very young then, what did I know? He died in Freetown in 1938, five years after I was born.

During the centenary of the Niger Diocese in the sixties my grandmother who was in her nineties then, and the only surviving grandchild of Adjai, was interviewed by the eminent Nigerian journalist, Babatunde Jose for the Nigerian Daily Times. Reminiscing about her life she told him that in 1868, her mother who was then expecting her, travelled from Freetown to Lagos to visit her parents, and as God would have it, she was born at Bishop's Court and baptised in Breadfruit Church in Lagos. She told him that in 1908 she was invited by her uncle, Archdeacon Dandeson Crowther, to come and assist him in Bonny in the educational aspects of his missionary work. He had planned to start a secondary school for Ibo girls, and she gladly accepted the invitation. She travelled to Lagos and thence to Bonny where she found the girls were eager to learn.

She went on, 'I nearly lost my two daughters Alice and Lina, due to the unfriendly climate. Times without number our house was flooded, but missionary work was interesting in those days in Bonny. I travelled about the creeks in canoes, and I still have a good recollection of the first church where all the services were conducted in Ibo. Sometimes when I read Nigerian newspapers, it gives me much pleasure that women's education, which my uncle and I started in Bonny, is yielding good results and that Ibo women are now playing an important role in the country's development. On this occasion of the centenary of the Niger Diocese, I send my sincere best wishes to the bishop, clergy, laity and all Christians in Nigeria. I am glad and thank God to be alive to see this day.'

This is not an academic, or scholarly study about the life of Adjai, written by a professional writer. Rather, it is a fond memoir, written by a journalist concerning our ancestor of whom we are all extremely proud. Someone who is now the patriarch and keeper of his flame within the family, and the chronicler of the family tree, which spans two hundred and five years, from the birth of Adjai in 1809, to the latest addition to the family in 2014. It is not even in chronological order, but aims to show the man and the era in which he lived, and the Christian mission work he did in places along the River Niger delta all these years ago.

When doing research for the book, I was surprised at some of the different accounts written about various aspects of his life and I became keen to find out what he wrote about himself. For example, there are several accounts either of how old he was when he was captured, or of the number of family members that were captured with him. One person said that he was married twice and had six children, which was far from the truth. He was married only once to Asano with whom he had six children, a marriage that lasted fifty years until she died in 1882. One report even stated that he was born in Zomba, Central Africa. I had to search extensively to find out the truth from the writings of the journals that he kept. Thankfully, he was a prolific journal keeper and letter writer, many carefully preserved in the archives of the Church Missionary Society, now at the Special Collection at Birmingham University. So, I have used extensive quotes from his letters and journals. But, although I searched diligently for it, I failed to find any references about his wife Asano. All I was able to find is that she shared the status of a slave girl, who like Adjai, had been rescued from a slave ship and brought to Freetown about the same time as Adjai. I failed to find out where she came from and from which tribe. A family member who is named Asano after her, thinks that she was a Fulani as the name Asano is of Fulani origin. My grandmother described her as being 'light-skinned' and having long black silky hair, tied in a bun at the back of her head, hair of which she was very proud. In his journals Adjai only mentioned her from time to time, calling her his helpmate, but about her background he said nothing. Some biographers have written that she was also an Oyo freed slave, and some that she was from the same tribe as Adjai, but all this is pure speculation. When researching the life of Sally Forbes Bonetta, the adopted daughter of Queen Victoria, I found that some writers called her Sarah, some Sara. But I have used Sally throughout as this is the name that Queen Victoria uses in her diary.

I also found that despite the racism he encountered from Europeans throughout his life, within and outside the church, which was mentioned by the Archbishop, there is not a hint of this in any of his writings; no mention of any snobbery or put down by his fellow European Christians. His faith in his God and his mission to spread His work amongst his own people was so strong that there was no room in his heart for any bitterness. And if he felt, or noticed it, and I am sure he did, he did not disclosed any of this in his journals. In fact, he expressed much gratitude that Europeans not only rescued him from slavery, but also provided his education and brought him to God. Of equal importance, I found out that although much has been written about his Saintliness and Christian faith, yet very little has been written about the monumental work he did in writing about, and translating whole sections of the Bible into the Yoruba and Nupe languages. And so I have listed some of the works he translated from English, at the end of the book.

I hope you enjoy reading about the life of Adjai, one of our greatest Africans who, after being saved from slavery, reached one of the highest positions in the Anglican church as a **'Bishop of the United Church of England and Ireland in the said countries in Western Africa beyond the limits of our dominion'.** After he died on New Year's Eve, 1891, the Anglican Church did not consecrate another African bishop until 1952, some sixty-one years later. Until then, Bishops were all white men.

Arnold Awoonor-Gordon
Chatham, Kent,
The United Kingdom

DEDICATION

This book is dedicated to the memory of Dr Olayiwola Celestin Akerele, former Manager of the Traditional Medicine Programme - World Health Organisation, Geneva 1935-2015 and Doctor Ameo Stella Adedevor. She died from the dreaded disease Ebola.

Dr Adedevor, Head of Operations, happened to be on duty at the Lagos-based First Consultant Medical Centre, when a patient, who had flown in from Monrovia in transit to the United States, fell ill at the airport arrived at the hospital for treatment. The patient had, in fact, contracted Ebola and Dr. Adedevor unknowingly caught the disease when she cared for him in the true traditions of her medical profession. She was the daughter of the Late Dr. Babatunde Kwake Adedevor, a renowned Harvard University-trained Physician and former Vice-Chancellor of the University of Lagos and great-great granddaughter of Bishop Samuel Adjai Crowther. She descended from his daughter Abigail and her husband the Rev. T. B. Macauley, and the great-great-granddaughter of Herbert Macauley, the foremost Nigerian politician, Father of Nationalism in the country who dominated Nigerian politics until his death. She was an active member of the Nigerian branch of the Crowther Descendants Family. She is sadly missed by her son and by the large and extended Crowther descendants in Nigeria, Ghana, Sierra Leone, Gambia and in the United Kingdom and the United States of America. May her soul rest in perfect peace.

CHAPTER 1
CAPTURE

On Sunday 30 June, 2014, a ceremony of **'thanksgiving and repentance'** was held in Canterbury Cathedral in order to mark the one hundred and fiftieth anniversary of the consecration of the first African Bishop in the Anglican Church. On that day, one hundred and fifty years ago, Samuel Adjai Crowther, the former African slave boy, made history by becoming the first African to be consecrated a Bishop.

At the ceremony the present Archbishop of Canterbury, The Most Reverend and Right Honourable Justin Welby, apologised for the ill-treatment of Crowther by the Anglican Church of England, as the first African bishop, and said that the service was one of **'thanksgiving and repentance. Thanksgiving for an extraordinary life, and repentance, shame and sorrow for Anglicans who are reminded of the sin of many of their ancestors'.**

Who was this man, the anniversary of whose consecration one hundred and fifty years ago, was being celebrated? He was Samuel Adjai Crowther, the African slave boy who became a Bishop.

Adjai was born in a place called Oshogun in what is today Oyo State of Nigeria, a few kilometres from Lseyin. He came from the Yoruba people who have traditionally occupied what is Western Nigeria.

His mother was called Afala, and came from a distinguished royal house. He had three sisters, the eldest was called Bola, then him, followed by Lanre and Amosa, who was a babe in arms at the time of his capture. There was another cousin living at the house. When it was time to be named at the traditional naming ceremony, he was given the name Adjai, which in the Yoruba language means 'one born with the umbilical cord round his neck'. We do not have any record as to the exact day or year in which he was born, but he himself claimed to have been born in 1809.

Here in his own words, is Adjai's account of what happened on that fateful day when he was captured: a letter written many years later to Rev. William Jewett, then Secretary to the Church Missionary Society in London dated February 1837 and sent from Fourah Bay in Freetown.

'Rev and Dear Sir,

As I think it will be interesting to you to know something of the conduct of providence in my being brought to the colony, where I have the happiness to enjoy the privilege of the Gospel, I give here a short account of it, hoping it may be excused, if I should prove rather tedious in some particulars.

I suppose sometime about the commencement of the year 1821, I was in my native country, enjoying the comfort of father and mother, and the affectionate love of brother and sisters. From that period I must date the unhappy, but which I am now taught in other respect to call blessed day, because it was the day in which I was violently turned out of my father's house, and separated from my relations, and in which I was made to experience what is called to be in slavery. With regard to its being called before, it being the day, which providence had marked out for me to set out in my journey from the land of heathenism, superstition and vice, to a place where the gospel is preached.

For some years, wars had been carried on in my Eyo-country, which was always attended with much devastation and bloodshed; the women, such men as had surrounded, or were caught with the children, were taken as captives. The enemies who carried on these wars, were principally the Eyo Mohammedans, with whom my country abounds, with the Foulahs, and such foreign slaves that had escaped from their owners, joined together, made a formidable force of about 20,000, who annoyed the whole country. They had no other employment, but selling slaves to the Spaniards and Portuguese on the coast.

The morning in which my town, Oshogun shared the same fate, which many others had experienced, was fair and delightful, and most of the inhabitants were engaged in their respective occupations. We were preparing breakfast without any apprehension, when about 9 a.m., a rumour was spread in the town, that the enemies had approached with intentions of hostility. It was not long after when they had almost surrounded the town, to prevent any escaped of the inhabitants; the town being rudely fortified with a wooden fence, about four miles circumference, containing about 12,000 inhabitants, which would produce 3,000 fighting men. The inhabitants not being duly prepared, some not being at home, those who were living about the gates to defend, as well as many weak places about the fence to guard against, and, to say in a few words, the men being surprised and therefore confounded, the enemies entered the town after about three or four hours resistance. There a most sorrowful scene imaginable was to be witnessed; women, some with three, four, or six children clinging to their arms, with the infants on their backs, and such baggage as they could carry on their heads, running as fast as they could through prickly shrubs, which, hooking their blies and other loads, threw them down from the heads from the bearers. While they found it impossible to go along with their loads, they endeavoured only to save themselves and their children: even these were impracticable with those who had many children to care for. While they were endeavouring to disentangle themselves from the shrubs, they were overtaken and caught by the enemies, with a noose of rope thrown over the neck of every individual, to be led in the manner of goats tied together under the direction of one man. In many cases a family was violently divided between three or four enemies who each took them away to see one another, no more.

Your humble servant was thus caught with his mother, two sisters, one infant, about 10 months old, and a cousin, while undertaking to escape from the enemies above described. My load consisted of nothing else than my bow and my fine arrows in the quiver; the bow I had lost in the shrub while I was extricating myself, before I could think of making any use of it against my enemies. The last view I had of my father was when he came from the fight to give us the signal to flee, he entered into our house, which was burned sometime back for some offence given by my father's adopted son. Hence, I never saw him more. Here I must take my leave, unhappy comfort life further.

Our conquers were Eyo Mohammedans, who led us away through the town. On our way, we met a man sadly wounded on the head, struggling between life and death. Before we got half way through the town, some Foulahs among the enemies, themselves violently separated my cousin from our number. Here also I must take my leave of my fellow captive cousin. His mother was living in another village. The town on fire, the houses being built with mud, some about twelve feet from the ground and high roofs in square form of different dimensions and spacious areas. Several of these belonged to one man, adjoined to, with passages communicating with each other. The flame was very high; we were led by my grandfather's house, already desolate, and in a few minutes after, we left the town to the memory of the flame, never to see, or enter it any more.

Farewell, the place of my birth, the play ground of my childhood and the place, which I thought would be the repository of my mortal body in old age. We were now out of Oshogun, going into a town called Isehi, about twenty miles from our town. On the way, we saw our grandmother at a distance with about three, or four of my other cousins taken with her, for a few minutes she was seen through the crowd to see her no more. Several other captives were held in the same manner as we were. Grandmothers, mothers, children, and cousins, were all taken captive. O sorrowful prospects - the aged women were to be greatly pitied, not being able to walk as fast as their children and grandchildren, they were often threatened with being put to death upon the spot, to get rid of them, if they would not go as fast as others and they were as often as wicked in their practice as in their words. O pitiful sight..whose heart would not bled to have seen this? Yes, such is the state of barbarity in the heathen land.

Evening came on, and coming to a spring of water, we drank a great quantity, which served us for breakfast, with a little roasted corn and dried meat, previously prepared by our victors for themselves.

During our march to Iseyin, we passed several other towns and villages, which had been reduced to ashes. It was almost midnight before we reached the town where we passed our doleful first night in bondage. It was not, perhaps, a mile from the walls of Iseyin while an old woman of about sixty was threatened in the manner above described. What had become of her, I could not learn.

On the next morning, our cords were being taken off our necks, we were brought to the Chief of our captors - for there were many other Chiefs - as trophies at his feet. In a little while, a separation took place; when my sister and I fell to the share of the Chief, and my mother and infant to the victors. We dared not vent our joy too loudly, but by heavy sobs. My mother, with the infant, was led away, comforted with the promise that she would see us again, when we should leave Iseyin for Dah'dah, the town of the Chief.

In a few hours after, it was soon agreed upon that I should be bartered for a horse in Iseyin, that very day. Thus I was separated from my mother and sister for the first time in my life, and the latter not to be seen more in this world. Thus, in the space of twenty-four hours, being deprived of liberty and all other comforts, I was made the property of three different persons. About the space of two months when the Chief was to leave Iseyin for his own town, the horse, which was then only taken on trial, not being approved of, I was restored to the Chief, who took me to Dah'dah, where I had the happiness to meet my mother and infant sister again with joy, which could be described by nothing else but tears of love and affection, and on the part of my infant sister with leaps of joy in a manner possible. Here, I lived for about three months amongst the horses, with my fellow captives. I now and then visited my mother and sister in our captors house without any fear, or thought of being separated any more.

At last, an unhappy evening arrived when I was sent with a man to get some money at a neighbourhood house. I went, but with some fear, for which I could not account and, to my great astonishment, in a few minutes I was added to the number of many other captives unfettered, to be led to the market town early the next morning. My sleep went from me; I spent almost the whole night in thinking of my dreadful situation, with tears and sobs, especially as my mother was in the same town, whom I had not visited a day or two back. There was another boy in the same situation with me; his mother was in Dah'dah. Being sleepy, I heard the first cock crow, the signal was given, when the traders arose, loaded the men slaves with baggage, and with one hand chained to their necks, we left the town. My little companion in affliction cried and begged much to be permitted to see his mother, but was soon silenced by punishment. Seeing this, I dared not speak, although I passed by the very house my mother was in. Thus, I became separated from my mother and sister, my then only comfort, to meet no more in this world of misery.

After a few days travel, we came to the market town of Ijahis. There I saw many who had escaped from our town to this place, or those who were in search of their relatives to set at liberty as many as they had the means of redeeming. There we were under very close inspection as there were many persons in search of their relations, and through that, many had escaped from their owners. In a few days, I was sold to a Mohammedan woman, with whom I traveled many towns in our way to the Popo country on the coast much resorted to by the Portuguese to buy slaves. When we left Injahi to Jo'ko. There, all spoke in the Ebwah dialect, but my mistress spoke Eyo, my own dialect. Here I was a perfect stranger, having far left behind the Eyo country. I lived in Jo'ko for about three months, walked about with my owner's son, with some degree of freedom, it being a place where my feet had never trod, and could I possibly make my way out through many a ruinous town and village we had passed, I should have soon become a prey to some others who would have gladly taken the advantage of me.

Besides, I could not think of going a mile out of the town alone at night, as there were many enormous devil-houses along the highway; and a woman having been lately publicly executed (fired at) being accused of witching her husband, who had died of a long tedious sickness. Five, or six heads of such persons as were executed for some crime or other, were to be nailed on the large tree in the market place to terrify others.

Now and then my mistress would speak with me and her son, that we should go to Popo country, where we should buy tobacco, and other fine things, to sell at our return. Now, thought I, this was the signal of my being sold to the Portuguese, who, they often told me during our *journey, were to be seen in that country. Being very thoughtful of this, my appetite forsook me, and in a few weeks I got the dysentery, which greatly preyed on me. I determined with myself that I would not go to the Popo country, but would make an end of myself, one way, or another. In several nights I attempted strangling myself with my hand; but had not the courage enough to close the noose tight, so as to effect my purpose. May the Lord forgive me this sin.*

I determined, next, that I would leap out of the canoe into the river, when we should cross it on our way to that country. Thus was I thinking when my owners, perceiving the great alteration which took place in me, sold me to some persons. Thus the Lord, while I knew him not, led me not into temptation, and delivered me from evil. After my price had been counted before my eyes, I was delivered to my new owners, with great grief and dejection of spirit, not knowing where I was now to be led. About the first cock crowing, which was the usual time to set out with the slaves to prevent their being much acquainted with the way, for fear of an escape should be made, we set out for Jabbo, the third dialect from mine.

After having arrived at Ik-ke-ku Yere, another town, we halted. In this place I renewed my attempt at strangling myself several times at night; but could not effect my purpose. It was very singular, that no thought of making use of knife entered my mind. However, it was not long before I was battered for tobacco, rum and other articles. I remained here in fetters, alone for some time, before my owner could get as many slaves as he wanted. He feigned to treat us more civilly, by allowing us to sip a few drops of white-man's liquor rum, which was so estimable an article, that none but Chiefs could pay for a jar of four, or five gallons; so remarkable it was, that no one should take breath before he swallowed every sip for fear of having the sting of his throat cut by the spirit of the liquor. This made it so much more valuable .

I had to remain alone, again, in another town in Jabbo, the name of which I do not now remember, for about two months. From here I was brought, after a few day walk, to a slave market, called I'ko-sy on the coast, on the bank of a large river which very probably was the Lagos on which we were afterwords captured.

The sight of the river terrified me exceedingly, for I had never seen anything like it in my life. The people on the opposite bank are called Eko. Before sunset, being battered again for tobacco, I became another commodity. Nothing terrified me more than the river, and the thought of going into another world. Cry was nothing now to vent my sorrow. My whole body became stiff. I was now made to enter the river to ford it to reach the canoe. Being fearful at my entering this extensive water, and being so cautious in every step I took, as if the next would bring me to the bottom, my motion was very awkward indeed. Night coming on and the men having very little time to spare, soon carried me into the canoe, and placed me among the corn bags, supplied me with one of my abalah for my dinner. Almost in the same position I was placed, I remained with my abalah in hand, quite confused in my thought, waiting every moment our arrival at the new world, which we did not till about four in the morning.

Here, I got once more into another dialect, the fourth from mine; if I may not call it altogether another language, on account of now and then, in some words, these being a faint shadow of my own. Here I must remark, that during the whole night voyage in the canoe, not a single thought of leaping into the river had entered my mind, but, on the contrary, the fear of the river occupied my thoughts,

Having now entered E'ko, I was permitted to go any way I pleased, there being no way of escaping on account of the river. In this place I met my two nephews, belonging to different masters. One part of the town was occupied by the Portuguese and Spaniards who had come to buy slaves. Although I was in Eko more than three months, I never once saw a white man; until one evening when they took a walk in company of about six, and came to the street of the house in which I was living. Even then I had not the boldness to appear distinctly to look at them, being always suspicious that they had come for me; for in a few days after, I was made the eighth in number of the slaves of the Portuguese. Being a veteran in slavery, if I may be allowed the expression, and having no more hope of ever going to my country again, I patiently took whatever came; although it was not without a great fear and trembling, that I received, for the first time, the touch of a white man, who examined me, whether I was young or not. Men and boys were at first chained together, with a chain of about six fathoms in length, thrust through in iron fetters on the neck of every individual, and fastened at both ends with padlocks. In this situation, the boys suffered the most; the men sometimes, getting angry, would draw the chain so violently, as seldom went without bruises on their little necks; especially the time to sleep, when they drew the chain so close to ease themselves of its weight, in order to be able to lay more conveniently, that we were almost suffocated or bruised to death, in a room with one door, which was soon fastened as we entered in; with no other passage of communicating the air, than the opening under the carved roof. They had also to suffer a great deal when they desired to get up at night to perform the office of nature, and the men were not willing to trouble themselves on their account.

Very often at night, when two or three quarrelled, or fought, the whole suffered punishment without any distinction. At least the boys had the happiness to be separated from the men, where their number was increased and no more chain to spare. We were grouped together by ourselves. Thus, were we going in and out, bathing together and so on. The female sex fared not much better. Thus, we were for nearly the space of four months.

About this time intelligence was given that the English were cruising the coast. This was another subject of sorrow with us. That there must be wars on the seas as well on the land, a thing never heard of before nor imagined practicable. This delayed our embarkation. In the meanwhile, the other slaves which were collected in Popo and was intended to be conveyed into the vessel the nearest way from this place, was brought into Eko amongst us. Among this number was Joseph Bartholomew, who later became my brother in the service of the Church Missionary Society.

After a few weeks delay, we were embarked, at night, in canoes from Eko to the beach; and on the following morning were embarked in the vessel, which immediately sailed away. The crew being busy embarking us, 187 in number, had no time to give us neither breakfast, nor supper, and we being unaccustomed to the motion of the vessel, employed the whole of this day in seasickness, which rendered a great part of us less fit to take any food whatsoever. On the very same evening, we were surprised by two English men-of-war; and on the next morning found ourselves in the hands of new conquerors, whom we at first dreaded, they being armed with long swords. In the morning, being called up from the hold, we were astonished to find ourselves among two very large men-of-war and several other brigs. The men-of-war, His Majesty's Ship

'Myrmidion' **Captain H. J. Leeke** and 'Iphigenia', Captain Sir Robert Mends, who captured us on 7 April, 1822, on the River Lagos.

Our owner was bound with his sailors, except the cook who was preparing our breakfast. Hunger rendered us bold, and not being threatened at first to get some fruits from the store, we in a short time took the liberty of ranging about the vessel in search of plunder of every kind. Now we began to entertain a good opinion of our new conquerors. Very soon after breakfast, we were divided into several of the vessels around us. This was now cause of new fears, not knowing where our misery would end. Being now, as it were, one family, we began to take leave of those who were first transported into the other vessels, not knowing what would become of them and ourselves. About this time we six intimate friends in affliction, among whom was my brother Joseph Bartholomew, kept very close together that we might be carried away at the same time. It was not long before we were conveyed to the 'Myrmidion,' in which we discovered not any trace of those who were transported before us. We soon came to the conclusion of what had become of them, when we saw parts of a hog hanging, the skin of which was white, a thing we had never seen before. For a hog was always roasted on fire to clean of the hair in my country, and a number of cannon shots arranged all along the deck. The former we supposed to be flesh, and the latter the head of the individuals who had been killed for meat. But we were soon undeceived by a close examination of the flesh with cloven feet, which resembled that of a hog, and a cautious approached to the shots that they were iron.

In a few days we were quite at home in the man-of-war, being only six in number we were soon selected by the sailors for their boys, and very soon furnished with dress. Our Portuguese owner and his son were brought over into the same vessel, bound in fetters, and thinking that I should no more get into his hands, I had the boldness to strike him on the head, while he was shaving by his son, an act, however, very wicked and unkind in its nature. His vessel was towed along by the man-of-war with the remainder of the slaves herein. But after a few weeks, the slaves being transported from her, and being stripped of her furniture, the Schooner was left alone on the ocean, destroyed at sea by captors, being found unworthy in consequence of being a bad sailor.

One of the brigs which contained a part of the slaves was wrecked on a sandbank. Happily, another vessel was nearby and all the slaves were saved. It was not long before another brig sunk during a tempest, with all the slaves and sailors, with the exception of about five of the latter, who were found in a boat after four or five days reduced to almost a few skeleton, and were so feeble they could not stand on their feet. 102 of our numbers were lost on this occasion.

After nearly two months and a half cruising on the coast, we were landed in Sierra Leone on

17 June, 1822. The same day we were sent to Bathurst, formally Leopold, under the care of Mr Davey. Here, we had the pleasure of meeting many of our country people, but none were known before. They offered us our liberty and freedom. We very soon believed them, but a few days after our arrival at Bathurst we had the satisfaction of being sent for at Freetown, to testify against our Portuguese owners, it being hinted to us that we should be delivered up to him again, notwithstanding all the persuasion of Mr Davey that we would return, we entirely refused to go ourselves, until we were carried. I could not but think of my ill conduct to our owners in the man-of-war. But, as time was passing away, and our consent could not be got, we were compelled to go by being whipped, and it was not a small joy to return to Bathurst again in the evening to our friends.

From this period I have been under the care of the C. M. Society, and in about six months after our arrival in Sierra Leone, I was able to read the New Testament with some degree of freedom, and was made a monitor, for which I was rewarded with four halfpenny per month. The Lord was pleased to hark back to those things which were spoken of by His servants, and being convinced that I was a sinner, and desired to obtain pardon through Jesus Christ, I was baptised on 11 December, 1825, by the Rev. J. Raban. I had the short privilege of visiting your happy and favoured land in the year 1826, in which it was my desire to remain for a year while to be qualified as a teacher to my fellow creatures, but providence ordered it so, that, at my return, I had wished for instructions under the tuition of the Rev. C. L. F. Haensel, who landed in Sierra Leone in 1827, through whose instrumentality I have been qualified so far as to be able to render some help in the service of the C. M. Society, to my fellow creatures. May I ever have a fresh desire to be engaged in the service of Christ, for it is 'Perfect Freedom.'

Thus, much I think necessary to acquaint you of the kindness of providence concerning me. Thus, the day of my captivity was to me a blessed day, when considered in this respect, though certainly it must be unhappy also, in my being deprived of it of my father, mother, sisters and all other relations. I must also remark, that I could not as yet find a dozen of Oshogun people from among the inhabitants of Sierra Leone.

I was married to a Christian lady on 21 September, 1829. She was captured by Her Majesty's Ship *Bann* under Captain Charles Phillips, on 31 October, 1822. Since then the Lord has blessed us with three children, a son and two daughters. As I doubt not it will be also acceptable to you whose paternal wish and desire for our improvement is inexpressible to know a little how a part of my time is employed, I hope it will not be looked upon as ostentation when I briefly mention the effect of Mr Hissling's advice on my study. I thankfully accept the offer of improvement held out to me by my being stationed here. At my coming to the institution to continue, I look on myself as a student rather on the one hand, while I endeavour to assist the pupils on the other, and I may humbly say that though the ministry and private assistance of Mr Hissling, I am greatly improved in many respects. My views of many things which were dark are set in a much clearer light, and when any difficulty arises in my cause of study, I always endeavour to avail myself of the opportunity of a living teacher, for which I sometimes prove troublesome to him. My studies which before were loose and unconnected, have been more stated and regular. When the plan of a regular study and its consequent effects had been pointed out to me, I immediately endeavoured to follow the experimental direction. I chose Doddridges' Family Exposition with which the paternal desire of the Rev. W. Harnsel for my improvement has furnished me, and which was pointed out to me by Mr. Hissling, or indeed a worthy book; I recommenced reading it regularly, at 6 o'clock, for one hour in the schoolroom, before our morning devotion. Though it was with some difficulty before I could bridle myself down to this plan, yet in a few weeks, when I began to see the thread of the four Gospels harmonised, at the same time comparing it with what was expanded at our morning devotion by Mr. Hessling, I soon began to perceive the privilege of a regular and stated study, and the beauty of the history of our Lord and Saviour.

When I had gone through the book, I was very much delighted with it, and being so poorly and scantly supplied with its rich and excellent contents, especially the epistolary part, that I hesitate not to give it a second regular perusal, which I am now perusing as far as the Revelation, with clear view and greater delight than formerly. Thus, I begin to experience what is quoted of Bishop Horne in the 'Companion to the Bible' when he said, with respect to the Psalms, 'These unfailing plants of paradise become as we are accustomed to them, still more and more beautiful, their blooms appear to be daily heightened, fresh odours are emitted, and new sweet are extracted from them, who hath once fasted their excellencies, will desire to cast them out again, and he who tastes them often, will relish them best.'

I hope I can pursue the study of the Holy Bible, without much mixture of weakness and swearing, which I often experience in so doing. May the Lord pardon my infirmities, ravings, and inequities in the reading of the Holy Word. That the time may come when the heathen shall be fully given to Christ for his inheritance, and the uttermost part of the earth for His profession, is my earnest prayer.

Yours humbly, thankfully,
and obedient servant

Samuel Crowther.

CHAPTER 2
DELIVERANCE

While Adjai was being transported in captivity away from his homeland, he did not know that far away in England in a place called the Palace of Westminster, his fate was being decided by a group of men with skins just like the Portuguese slavers who were holding him captive in the dank hold of the slave ship. For a group of men, whose names he was to get to know and hold in great esteem, were debating the abolition of the slave trade. Members of the Abolitionist Movement, for over twenty years, had tried to convince Parliament to pass an Act to end this inhuman trade. These brave men eventually succeeded and in 1807 the British Government passed the Act, which made slavery illegal including the buying, selling and transporting of people.

The main players in the abolition of the slave trade in England were William Wilberforce, Granville Sharp, brothers John and Henry Thornton, Thomas Clarkson and Hannah More. They were known as the 'Clapham Sect,' sometimes known as the 'Clapham saints' as they all lived in, or around Clapham Common, in south London; who were members of Holy Trinity, a Georgian church on Clapham Common, still standing proudly today as it did all those years ago. They all played their several parts in the eventual abolition of the slave trade, and their names are engraved today on the walls of the church. Granville Sharp was a Civil Servant, the Thornton brothers, being wealthy, provided the much needed funds and the meeting place. Clarkson went all over the country collecting records, and Hannah More, a well known playwright brought her popularity to the cause, and wrote the following words in her famous poem entitled Slavery:

> *What page of human annals can record*
> *A deed so bright as human rights restored,*
> *O may that God-like deed, that shining page,*
> *Redeem our fame, and consecrate our age.*

Hannah More died in 1833 aged 88.

Granville Sharp was a civil servant, working as a junior clerk in the Ordinance Office, who was to become an advocate for the abolition of the slave trade by a chance encounter he had, which was to change his life. In 1765 he had come across a young slave boy by the name of Jonathan Stronge, who had been cruelly beaten by his master David Lisle of Barbados, and left on a London street to die. Granville Sharp took the poor boy to St. Barts Hospital and paid for him to be treated. He eventually got better and with the help of Sharpe, he secured a job working for an apothecary. Two years later, the boy was abducted by his original master and sold to a slave owner from Jamaica. He appealed to Granville Sharp, who without any legal training, fought the case in court and won. This was the turning point in his life and for the next fifty years he dedicated himself to the abolitionist cause. He acted for several slaves, over the years, winning some and losing some. He died 1n 1813 at the age of seventy-eight. He did not live to see the passing of the Act, which he had fought against for so long.

Although today the people have forgotten the names of some of the people who fought for the abolition of the slave trade, William Wilberforce is fondly remembered for spearheading the movement as a Member of Parliament through his friendship with the Prime Minister, William Pitt the Younger. Wilberforce also persuaded Josiah Wedgwood, the pottery maker, to design a medallion of a black slave in chains on his knees with the inscription - **'Am I not a man and brother,'** which sold widely to raise funds for the cause. He later had it put on dinner plates in order to start the discussions about the slave trade. It has been noted that this small group of people brought a change that had a long lasting effect on the people of England. It is interesting to note that William Wilberforce died died on 29 July, 1853, just three days after Parliament passed the Act that abolished the slave trade in the United Kingdom. He must have died a very happy man to know that what he and the others had championed for many years had eventually come to pass.

But, slaves already owned by their masters, remained slaves in England, and it was not until 1833 with the passing of the Slavery Abolition Act that all slaves became free. This was followed in 1838 by a ban on false apprenticeship schemes, giving true freedom to all slaves. All these acts came about after Parliament had been reformed and two-thirds of those who had supported slavery had been swept from power.

But, long before the Act of Abolition was passed, both public opinion in Britain and in particular the Abolition Society had taken a great interest in the slaves. Mainly because there were hundreds of them living in wretched conditions, in London and in ports like Bristol, Liverpool and Portsmouth. In 1772, Granville Sharp obtained the now famous judgment by Lord Justice Mansfield, which decreed that: As soon as ever any slave should set foot upon English territory he became free. Granville Sharp with the assistant of Thomas Clarkson, the Member of Parliament William Wilberforce, the Quakers and the Methodists, then began the struggle for the complete destruction of the slave trade and to help those who had set foot in England and were, therefore, free. The Committee for the Black Poor was formed to look after the freed slaves who were living destitute in the country. That was why slaves in the United States of America escaped to Nova Scotia in Canada, which was then a British territory, and found freedom there.

But, despite the abolition of the slave trade by Britain, other European countries, especially the Portuguese, carried on the trade with renewed vengeance. So, the British decided to deploy a fleet of British Naval ships based in Bathurst, Gambia and designated the *West African Squadron* with a specific mission to intercept all slave ships.

THE WEST AFRICAN SQUADRON

The squadron patrolled the coast of West Africa between 1808 and 1860 when the trade was finally abolished. And so one morning in 1821, the British frigates *Myrmidon* under Captain Harry Leeke and the *Iphigenia* under Captain Charles Mends, sailing from Bathurst, spotted a ship, the *Esperanza Felix*, belonging to Manuel Jose Freire, a notorious Brazilian slaver. It was given a signal to stop. It didn't at first, but the two frigates soon caught up with it. A party boarded the ship and found the hold crowded with 187 slaves including the young boy, Adjai. Although the Portuguese captain protested strongly, his protests were ignored and the slaves were transferred to the British Naval ships. One can only imagine the relief of the slaves at being freed, treated kindly by these new people, given food to eat and water to drink, and new clothes, and being in the fresh sea air for the first time, away from the dank and filthy hold of the ship that had enslaved them. After Adjai and the other slaves were rescued from their Portuguese slavers, they were taken to Freetown, in the new colony of Sierra Leone, arriving on 17 June,1822. They landed in what became known as King Jimmy Wharf, which is today King Jimmy market, where people from Bullom, on the opposite side of the river, bring their produce to sell.

The country had been named *Sierra Leone* by the Portuguese Navigator, Pedro da Cintra, when he called there to water his ships in 1462. It is said that he arrived during the rainy season, and seeing the shape of the mountain, which he mistook for a crouching lion, and hearing the roar of thunder, which is prevalent at that time of the year, he gave the country the name *Sierra Leone*, meaning Lion Mountain in the Portuguese language. The natives called it simply 'Romarong,' or 'Mountain' in their language. It is said that Sir John Hawkins also used the port for watering his ships. Several European nations, including Britain took part in the slave trade, and it is stated that even Queen Elizabeth1, participated in the trade by providing a ship for the slave-trading voyage by Sir John Hawkins, which brought him to this place to water his ships during the Elizabethan age.

The question now arose as to what to do with all the slaves in England who had been freed under the Lord Justice Mansfield Act of 1772. They were a notable sight living on the streets of London, Liverpool, Bristol and several cities, most of them in a pitiful condition and they soon became known as **'The Black Poor.'** The name was coined and given to the community of black people, some of whom had been brought to England, either as slaves who had escaped, or sometimes as indentured servants who had served on ships as seamen then released after their service. Their situation inspired several prominent citizens to set up a charitable organisation in 1786 with the quaint name of *'The Committee for the Relief of the Black Poor,' to* provide help, assistance and sustenance to the distressed peoples of African and Asian origin living on the streets of London. They held their first meeting on 10th January,1786 at the premises of Mr Faulder, a book seller in Bond street and the second in Batson's Coffee House, opposite the Royal Exchange. These meetings attracted some very prominent figures from London's financial elite, such as George Peters, Governor of the Bank of England, a noted Philanthropist and, surprisingly also a slave owner; John Julius Angerstein, General Robert Melville, the abolitionists Samuel Hoare, two of the three Thornton brothers, Henry and Samuel, and James Petit Andrews and Sir Joseph Andrews, all very prominent in London society. They became the founder members of the charitable foundation and soon launched an appeal for funds which, when it closed on April 18 only three months later, had raised the colossal sum of £890.1s as reported by the Morning Herald in its issue of February 14:

'The example of the Duchess of Devonshire, in contributing to the relief of the poor Blacks, had a salutary effect. The Countess of Salisbury, the Countess of Essex, Marchioness of Buckingham and a variety of other titled characters were also on the charitable list. Other donors included many clergy, bishops and Members of Parliament, including William Pitt.

But, the largest donation came from the Quakers.'

Two centres were opened in London for the regular distribution of the funds collected. One in Mile End in the East End, and the other in Lisson Grove, Marylebone in central London. Each centre was opened for several hours each day to provide outdoor relief. The committee were also able to set up a sick house in Warren street, to provide for 40 to 50 men needing medical attention. They also provided clothes for men needing to obtain work as sailors and seamen. But, as there was a shortage of work, the city was soon full of the unemployed black poor, and the committee were instrumental in the transfer of the Black poor to Sierra Leone. Historians are divided, as is usual amongst experts, whether it was a desire to remove the black people who were seen as nuisance in the streets of London and other British cities, or was it more focused on strictly altruistic goals. We shall never know.

But, it was at the suggestion of Granville Sharp and Dr. Henry Smeathman, a Swedish botanist and entomologist who had spent some time on the West African coast, that a plan was arranged for *'A settlement to be made in Sierra Leone on the grain coast of West Africa, intended more particularly for the service and happy establishment of Blacks and People of Colour, to be shipped as freemen under the direction of the Committee for Relieving of the Black Poor and under the protection of the British Government.'*

GRANVILLE SHARP TENDING TO
JONATHAN STRONG, WHOM HE FOUND
NEAR DEATH ON THE STREET IN LONDON

The government gave £12 per black person towards the cost, and The Abolition Society bought three ships the *Belisarius, Atlantic* and *Vernon*. They set sail from Plymouth Freetown on 9 April, where the liberated slaves were to be settled, under the protection of a British Naval Man-of-War *HMS Nautilus, and carried* 280 freed black men, 41 black women and 70 white women. Some of these white women were married to the black freed man, but the others were women of the town, whom, according to myth, is said came on board when the bars and alleyways of the city of Plymouth were scouted, and encouraged, or shanghaied, to make the journey. What they thought of this adventure when they realised their true fate and destination, is not recorded. But, it is said that they became the founding mothers of Freetown.

This motley band of people arrived in what Granville called the **Province of Freedom,** a place that from then on became known as Freetown. It was then, and today, still one of the three most natural harbours in the world. Not all the men made it to the promised land; eighty-five died on the way. It is said that when the first settlers arrived at their new home, they gathered at the foot of the giant Cotton Tree and held their first prayer meeting to give thanks to God for bringing them safely to the new land. The Cotton Tree still stands in the centre of Freetown until today. It is interesting to note that after the ship sailed the Committee for the Black Poor, washed their collective hands, dissolved itself, as if they had done their best for the poor blacks crowding the streets on England's major cities. The members moved on to find other philanthropic causes to take up their time.

The COTTON TREE - FREETOWN

The men who sailed to Freetown had to sign what was called **The Frankpledge,** the essential characteristic of which was the law of compulsory sharing of the responsibility in all matters, legal or otherwise, amongst the members of the community. The land they settled on was bought from King Tom, the local chief of the Temne people. There is a story that the land was bought for £25 and a bolt of red cloth. But, according to records the payment to King Tom, from whom they purchased twenty-square miles of land, did include some cloth, other goods, rum and hats. The land was ceded to the Crown on 22 August, 1792 for the purpose of establishing a free community of British subjects. That same year, the British Government brought over one thousand freed slaves from Nova Scotia in Canada who had settled there after the American War of Independence. The town was given the name of *Freetown,* in recognition of the freedom the former slave enjoyed. In 1791,The Sierra Leone Company had been formed with Wilberforce, Clarkson and

Sharp, three of the directors. In 1804 two German Lutherans were sent by the company to Freetown, but they soon died as at that time the place was not suitable for Europeans. Wilberforce himself died in 1831.

WILLIAM WILBERFORCE

Here, we must pay tribute to John Wesley, one of the founders of Methodism, who with his brother William, and George Whitfield, formed a triumvirate of great evangelists and preachers, who all denounced the slave trade from their chapel in City Road in London. In fact John Wesley, few days before he died, wrote a letter to William Wilberforce, urging him to persevere in this great endeavour. He wrote 'Go on in the name of God and in the power of His might, until even American slavery, the vilest that ever saw the sun, shall vanish away before it.'

Here also, tribute must be paid to the Society of Friends, the Quakers. They presented the first petition to the House of Commons, praying that something might be done to ameliorate the shocking practice of slavery. So, with the backing of such important, distinguished and influential group of people, it is no wonder that victory was achieved, when on 25th March, 1807, the Bill for the Abolition of the British Slave Trade became law. This was just one step forwards. The next step was what to do with the free slaves who were roaming the cities of England. It was then that the Granville plan to settle them in Freetown was put in place.

So, when Adjai and the other slaves were rescued from their Portuguese slavers, they were brought to Freetown, arriving on 17 June, 1822, to the new colony of Sierra Leone. The first settlers as mentioned above, had arrived in 1787. But, soon after they arrived, anarchy, disease, disorder, mutinies, quarrelling, infighting, stealing and aggression from the natives soon set in. Also there was an attack by the French, who invaded the town carrying off all they could lay their hands on. Resentment became the order of the day, and the deteriorating morale of these first settlers became the concern of the God fearing people of goodwill in England, who had sent them out there in the first place. It was due to the zeal and discipline of the

Governor Zachary Macauley, the father of the historian, that order was restored.

The Church Missionary Society (CMS) without then knowing it, was to play a very decisive role in the story of the slave boy Adjai, and in Sierra Leone in particular, for the next two hundred years, or so. The society was founded on 12 April, 1799 in England by a group of twenty-five Clergymen and Laymen, all good Christian men, who met in the upper chamber of the Castle and Falcon Inn, Aldersgate in London. The resolution they passed at the meeting stated that *'it is the duty highly incumbent upon every Christian to endeavour to propagate the knowledge of the Gospel among heathen.'* The purpose was the sending out of missionaries to *'Christianise the heathen peoples of the world, especially in Africa.'* The society had some fundamental missionary principles, which were to be the guidelines of its work throughout the years. These were:

> *To follow God in the same way as*
> *missionaries of the early church;*
> *To begin humbly and on a small scale;*
> *To put money after prayer and study, and*
> *To depend on the Holy Spirit.*

The reason they focused on Africa at the outset, was that they felt strongly about the wrongs that Europeans had brought to the continent, with the wicked and inhuman commerce of the slave trade. They were anxious to make atonement for it. They were to do this by taking the bible to the heathen Africans, to tell them 'where the wicked cease from troubling, and the slave is free from his master'. It soon became one of the largest and most influential Christian missionary institutions in the world. But, it took many years before they could recruit men who were brave enough to venture into what was then regarded as *'the Dark Continent'*. The society held its first Committee meeting in 1812 at its headquarters in Salisbury Square in London. This remained the headquarters until 1966 when they moved to Waterloo Road; later in 2005, the Trustees announced its move to Oxford. In 1841 the Rev. Henry Venn was appointed its secretary and ran the society until his death in 1873. It can be said that Henry Venn guided and expanded the work of the society, and was the staunch supporter of Adjai throughout his life.

But, even though the society was to begin work as soon as it was formed, yet it had some difficulties doing so. For it could not start its work until it had received the nod from Archbishop John Moore (1783-1805) the then Archbishop of Canterbury, who after sixteen months delay came back with these famous words *'that he would look on the proceedings with candour and that it would give him pleasure to find them such as he could approve.'* At the time it seems as if he, and other Church of England leaders did not see the need for another missionary society. It was not until the year 1815 during the time of Archbishop Charles Manners-Sutton (1805-1828) that a bishop of the church gave formal approval of the society. The society had no difficulty in choosing Sierra Leone as the first place in which to start work, for Freetown by then had been a colony and a settled community for freed slaves since 1786.

The founders of the CMS had difficulty though, in recruiting English men to go out as missionaries. Many were interviewed but all were found wanting and not to have the right temperament that they were looking for. It was not until 1808 that they were able to find two German Lutheran missionaries to send to the new colony to *Evangelise, Christianise* and bring order to what were then seen as a pagan people. One must admit that the arrival of the Missionaries did bring some form of order to a place that before had been disorderly. The first two missionaries were the Rev Melchior Renner and Peter Hartweg, two Germans trained in the seminary in Berlin who went out in 1808, but soon moved to Rio Pongos. In 1809 the Rev Gustavus Reinhold Nylander, another German missionary, went out to Freetown and acted as Government Chaplain. Over the next six years nine other Missionaries, all Germans with English wives, were sent out.

Initially, the CMS granted prime importance to Education, in line with evangelism. So, when the society received a grant of eleven hundred acres of land on Leicester mountain outside Freetown, a Christian Institution was erected in 1815, and by the following year three hundred and fifty children were being educated there. The boys receiving instructions in various trades, and the girls in such occupations as were suited to their sex. But the evangelising side was not neglected, and the gospel and praying was also of great importance.

There was a marked line of demarcation between the various groups who made up the population of Freetown. There were the freed slaves from England, who were the original 'settlers', the liberated slaves who were 're-captives', like Adjai, who had been 'liberated' and set free from slave ships, and the 'Nova Scotians' who had arrived from Canada after the end of the American war of Independence. Later, five hundred and fifty 'Maroons' arrived from Jamaica to swell the population. So, people identified themselves either as *Settlers, Re-captives, Nova Scotians or Maroons*. The Maroons were mostly people originally from Ashanti in Ghana, who had been captured and sent to Jamaica. The four sets of people did not mix, and had their own churches, schools and cultures. It took many many years before they were able to mix and to inter-marry between the four groups of people. They then became known as Creoles. But, as Freetown grew, prospered and expanded, the town

was elevated, and on 9 January, 1817 the Governor, Sir Charles MacCarthy laid the foundation stone of St Georges Church, which later became a Cathedral in 1852 when it became a diocese. The first bishop was an Englishman, Bishop Vidal.

St GEORGE'S CATHEDRAL

The church built by the Maroons still stands between Liverpool and Percival streets in the centre of the town, and descendants of the original people who built it, still worship there.

MAROON CHURCH

Adjai was amongst a large number of children who were brought to Freetown, either as settlers or re-captives. In order to accommodate them, the CMS built a home where these children were to be housed and given a Christian education. Some however, were sent to live with Christian families, as was Adjai. He was sent to live with Mr and Mrs Davey, two missionary teachers, in one of the mountain villages called Bathurst. Two other Christian friends of the Davey's, Mr and Mrs John Weeks also became interested in this young boy and willingly helped with his education. Also living with the Davey's at the same time as Adjai, was a young liberated girl called Asano. She had been rescued by Her Majesty's ship 'Bann,' under Captain Charles Phillips, on 31 October, 1822 and landed in Freetown the same year as Adjai. They studied together, learned to read and write, went to school, quote from the bible and say their prayers.

We read from his journals what went through the mind of Adjai, who within a short period of a few years of his life, had been taken from his home and family, marched to the coast, shackled on a ship, rescued from a fate he could not contemplate, and here he was amongst white people, who for the first time showed him much kindness. He also thought of his mother and his family from time to time. But, he was a very smart boy, and soon was fluent in the English language and could read and write it fluently, helped by his new guardians. This was due not only to the spiritual and practical educational practices put in place by the CMS, whereby the young people under its auspices were not only taught to read and write, but also trained in manual labour. Therefore, the young men were trained in the skills of carpentry, house building, shoe making, and the girls in housekeeping and cooking, skills that they would find useful as they grew older and went out into the wider world.

Under the influence of his kind guardians, Adjai grew in stature and all were pleased with the progress he made over the years. He attended church on a regular basis and was allowed sometimes to read the scriptures during the service. On the eleventh of December in 1825, when it was deduced that he must be about sixteen, he was received into the Christian church and baptised by the Reverend John Rahan of the CMS. He kept his original African name of Adjai, but was given the names Samuel Crowther, after a venerable clergyman, the Rev. Samuel Crowther, vicar of Christ Church, Newgate Street, London, and one of the committee members of the Church Missionary Society in London. The name was chosen for him by his new guardian Mrs Davey, who had been a Sunday school teacher at the church before coming to Sierra Leone. Other re-captives and liberated slaves also took English names when they were baptised and until today there, are British family names such as Williams, Davies, Allen, Willoughby and Gordon in Freetown. The names of the streets such as Walpole, Trelawney, Bathurst, Liverpool, Wellington and Wilberforce also reflect the fact that this was once a British colony. Similarly, names of the villages around Freetown such as Charlotte, Gloucester, Regent, Waterloo and Leicester maintained those colonial links.

In the year 1826, we can only assume, that to show off one of the successes of the CMS in Sierra Leone, he was invited to accompany Mr. and Mrs. Davey on the slow boat journey to England, where they were to attend a meeting of the society. They reached Portsmouth on 16 August, 1826, and soon afterwards he was paraded and showed off at the London meeting, and at various other meetings in the homes of some of the sponsors of the society. Later he was enrolled at the Parochial school in Liverpool Street, Islington, north London for the remainder of his stay. While studying at the college, he lodged at the home of the Rev. E. Bickesteth. One can imagine how he felt when winter came with its cold and snow, which he must have been amazed to witness for the first time. In a letter Adjai wrote later to one of the people he met in England. He says, *I had the privilege of visiting your happy and favoured land in 1826, in which it was my desire to remain for a good while to be qualified as a teacher to my fellow-creatures.'*

After a year's sojourn in London, he and his guardians returned to Freetown. As soon as he arrived, he was appointed Assistant Master at Regent school with an annual salary of £24. For a young man such as Adjai, this was remuneration beyond his wildest dream, and was the very first money he earned in his life. Later he moved to Gloucester as Assistant Master at an increase in his annual salary. On his return from England he was a reunited with Asano, the young girl with whom he had studied when they both lived with Mr & Mrs Davey. She had also been baptised and took the names of Susan Thompson, but retained her African name of Asano.

There is very little in various documents I researched about the background of Asano, but in his book, 'A Patriot to the End, Bishop Ajayi Crowther,' Professor J. E. Ade-Ajayi states on page 56 that there is a tradition that she was the granddaughter of Alafin Atiba, the first Alafin at present day Oyo (through her mother, Siye.) But, a family member who also has the name Asano, says that the name is of Fulani origin. Although I can find no photo of Asano, my grandmother, who knew her well, told me that she had very fair skin and had long very black glossy hair, which she always wore in a bun at the back of her head.

Now we come to an important junction in the life of Adjai, for we read in the minutes of a meeting at the CMS council held in London that '**An application from Samuel Crowther, schoolmaster at Regent, for leave to enter matrimony with Susan Thompson of Bathurst, having been submitted and a satisfactory account being received of the girl's suitableness for a fellow-worker with him, it was resolved that this meeting consent to the marriage of Samuel Crowther and Susan Thompson taking place.**'

Adjai wasted no time and the wedding took place as soon as approval was received from London, much to the delight and blessings of their guardians. And so they were married. They stayed together for over fifty years until her death on 18 October, 1880. The union was blessed with six children. Abigail, born on 6th March 1836, Josiah born in 1838, Samuel born on 5 August, 1840, Susan born on 14 October, 1844, and Juliana and Dandeson Coates in 1846. One son died soon after being born. Before she died in 1881 Asano (my grandmother told me that her grandchildren always referred to to her as 'Grandma Asano' and he as 'Grandpa Adjai') lived long enough to see her family expand to the second and third generations.

The girls all married clergymen. Abigail married the Reverend Thomas Barbington Macauley, founder and first principal of Lagos Grammar School and were the parents of Herbert Macauley the veteran Nigerian politician. Susan married the Reverend George Pompey Nicol, chaplain to the forces in the Gambia, and the parents of my grandmother, and Juliana married the Reverend Charles Thompson. Their son Dandeson Coates, followed in his father's footsteps and became a priest. At one time he served as Archdeacon in his father's diocese. Samuel studied medicine and science, but did not practice and later turned to trade. Josiah the youngest son did industrial training in Manchester and became a businessman. Although Dandeson married, he did not have any children, and the other two sons also never had any children to carry on the Crowther name. This my grandmother told me, was a disappointment to her grandfather. But he took heart that Susan added Crowther to her married name, and which became Crowther-Nicol. And Juliana also added Crowther to her married name of Thompson. This has continued down that line to the present day. Thus, the Crowther name lives on today in various forms within his direct family line. There are Crowther-Nicol's and Crowther-Marke's around in the family, and there is a Samuel Crowther-Marke and his brother Adjai

Crowther-Marke, living with their parents, the Melville Crowther-Marke's in Australia.

Adjai was keen to have his children educated to the highest standard by sending them to England to study. Thus, in one of his journals we read that he applied to the CMS to send his sons to England for at least a year, with him paying their fees and expenses by quarterly instalments from his salary. *'We shall feel highly delighted that we have afforded our children the opportunity of seeing something of the world, and of associating with a people of higher principle, that on their return to Africa they may prove a blessing in what state of life it may please God to call them. We wish them to return to Sierra Leone when they have completed their education.*

CHAPTER 3
STUDENT AND MARRIED LIFE

On Christmas Day 1827, Adjai became the first student to enter the doors of what was originally called the African Institute, later to become known as Fourah Bay College, the Christian institution that the CMS founded for the training of local priests. The English lady traveller Mary Kingsley, was to infer snootily, that the institute was setup to train **'Negros in trousers to spread Western civilisation and at the same time Christianity'.** The institute had been setup in order to train native priests to take over from European priests, whose numbers were decimated by malaria and other tropical diseases, soon after they arrived in the country. The building chosen on Fourah Bay on the Eastern side of Freetown, is still standing today, although in a rather dilapidated condition. Being designed by an architect in England, who had never set foot on African soil, it had a library, lecture rooms, kitchens, dining room and a dormitory for the students. But, in a wry humour, every room had a coal burning fireplace, which was out of place when one considered that the temperature was about 90 degrees, even in the shade. But that did not stop the students studying for their BA and MA degrees, when the institution became affiliated with the University of Durham in England from 1876 until it became a fully fledged university in 1967. The setting up of the institution had the full support of the Irish-born Governor, Brigadier-General Charles Macarthy (1764-1824), who was very keen in the education of native children.

FOURAH BAY COLLEGE - CLINE TOWN

The founding of the institution was in the nature of an experiment by the CMS who were fortunate in their selection of the first principal. He was a young German-born Lutheran missionary, trained at the Basle Seminary, who proved a very wise choice; a brilliant Bavarian clergyman, the Reverend Charles L. F. Haensel. He brought strict Germanic discipline to the institute, and his remit from the CMS in London was to train native teachers and priests to replace the high rate of mortality amongst the British missionaries who were dying from the scourge of malaria and black water fever in large numbers. It was said that the life span of a British missionary in the colony was one year. As a result, Sierra Leone got the name **'the white man's grave'** as so many white men died there. One of the bishops was later to write, *'The churchyard at Kissy with its multiplied memories of those not lost, but* *gone before, is a silent but eloquent witness to the kind of schooling, which missionaries for Africa requires.'*

As the Africans seem to be immuned to the bite of the insects that carried the diseases, it was felt that they should be trained to carry on the Christian work of the CMS. Adjai, being well educated with a British education to boot, following his stint at the Parochial school in Islington, was earmarked early to be trained as a priest. His name was the first on the register of the first six local youths to enter the institution.

Adjai had to make some scarifies in order to enter the institution to become better educated. One of this was losing his salary as a schoolmaster. Another was as a recently married man, he would miss his new wife. It is interesting to see another sacrifice he had to make from a letter written by his Principal, the Rev. Haensel in which he says, **'When Samuel Crowther first entered the institution he brought with him a mattress he had been given in England, but as this was too great a luxury, I at once forbade its entrance, to which he readily consented.'** *'But,'* he added, *'I wish for the good of his own soul to see him in this state of lowliness of mind, which Africans so easily lose by visits to England.'* Just shows what was thought about Africans at that time. But although we can only imagine what Adjai thought of parting with his prized possession at the time and what he must have thought about this high handed attitude of the Principal, we shall never know. For, he never mentioned this incident in any of his journals and letters.

Adjai was enrolled at the institute as a probationer in the first instance, because, according to a report to the CMS in London by the principal, *'This is owing to the information which is received of an attachment entertained by him towards a girl who is schoolmistress at Bathurst. He says he will not let it interfere with his education and I am ready to trust his sincerity, but it is to be doubted whether he knows it himself sufficiently; and it will be easier to let him withdraw during this period of probation if he should feel it is too hard to be separated from her than after his full reception as a full student.'*

But, the principal need not have worried about the dedication of Adjai to obtain the type of education that he knew would stand him in good stead later in life. He made rapid progress through the college and was soon made a monitor by the Principal. Several years later, reminiscing about his time at the institute and the influence that the principal had on him, he was to write, *'Mr. Haensel was a peculiar person altogether; we could never find one to match him. He was venerated by all the merchants, they would all tremble at his presence, if they did not act straightforwardly, or honestly. He would tell you in a language, which was not offensive, but which you would not forget and next time you saw him you would tremble to act in the same way, either by speaking inadvertently, or by acting contrary to Christian* *principles. He was a man of penetra*ting qualifications.'

Student life for a married man could not have been easy. The students were given a couple of shirts, a pair of trousers, a hat and a jacket. With a book of common prayer and a bible, this made up their entire possessions. After a month, or so, they were given another pair of trousers and another jacket and this was for their full dress on Sundays and other special occasions. At home the students went barefoot, and it took them all a while to get used to wearing shoes.

Adjai graduated from the institution in 1830, when he was about twenty-four and was appointed Headmaster of a school in the mountain village of Regent. His wife was also appointed Headmistress. He did an excellent job at the school, and found time to read Greek and Latin, which had been taught at the institute. He also took prayer meetings and bible teaching and assisted the missionary John Weeks, who first looked after him when he was brought off the ship, with bible classes and Sunday School, teaching the holy Gospel and spreading the word of God. Mr Weeks mentioned him in a letter to a friend, *'I have now a good assistant in Samuel Crowther; the Lord give him grace and keep him humble.'* He was so good at teaching that he was promoted to a much larger school at Wellington Village.

When the Reverend Charles Haensel returned to Europe at the end of his success in establishing and growing the institute, he was replaced by the Rev. G. A. Kissling as principal. Soon after taking up his duties, and looking round for someone to appoint as Assistant teacher at the college, Adjai was the obvious choice. He recommended him to the CMS in London, and Adjai received a letter offering him the post in 1834. Although his wife was a little sceptical about him taking up the appointment, he was able to persuade her that it was an opportunity that he could not pass up. So, within a short period of time he had enrolled at the institute, graduated from it, become Headmaster of the school at Regent and Wellington, and now he was back again as an Assistant Teacher at his Alma mater. How proud he must have felt. But all this he owed to his Christian God, as himself wrote many years later. *'From this period I must date the unhappy, but which I am ever taught in other respect to call blessed day, which I shall never forget in my life. I call it an unhappy day, because it was the day on which I was violently turned out of my father's house and separated from my relatives and in which I was made to experience what is called to be in slavery. With regard to its being called blessed it was the day which Providence had marked out for me to set out on my journey from the land of heathenism, superstition and vice, to a place where the Gospel is preached.'*

During his time at the institute he found time to brush up on his Latin and Greek, and to mentor some of the students. One such was George Pompey Nicol, who later became his son-in-law when he married his eldest daughter Susan, and became Chaplain to the Forces in the Gambia. They were the parents of my Grandmother Emilie.

During his time at Fourah Bay College, when the principal had to return to England for a brief period, Adjai was put in charge, which means that he was the first African to head this august institution. In 1845 the CMS opened the Church Missionary Society Grammar School in Freetown to provide secondary school education for young boys, not only for boys in the country but from all over West Africa. In 1849 the Female Institution, later to become the Annie Walsh Memorial School, was started by the society for the secondary education of girls under the formidable Miss Sass.

CHAPTER 4
MISSIONARY EXPLORER

In the year 1841, the British government and the Society for the Extinction of the Slave Trade, organised an expedition to sail up and explore the river Niger, one of the longest rivers in West Africa, which empties itself in the Niger basin in the East of Nigeria. The aim of the expedition was three fold. One was to try to put an end to the slave trade, which was still rife in the area; two, was to open the area to trade and commerce and the third was to spread the Christian gospel. Three ships made up the expedition; the *Albert,* named after Prince Albert, Consort of Queen Victoria, the *Wilberforce,* named after the great abolitionist William Wilberforce and the *Soudan,* named after one of the branches of the River Niger. Lord John Russell, Colonial Secretary, in order to obtain funds for the expedition, explained to the Treasury that such an expedition would open up new fields for commerce which would benefit the Government, and at the same time help to put an end to the slave trade. In a letter to the Treasury he wrote, *'The Queen has directed her ministers to negotiate conventions and agreements with those chiefs and powers, the basis of which conventions would be, first, the abandonment and absolute prohibition of the slave trade; and secondly, the admission, for consumption in this country on favourable terms, of goods, the produce and manufacture of the territories, subject to them - of those chiefs the most considerable over the countries adjacent to the Niger and its tributary streams.'*

The setting up of such an expedition soon came to the attention of the Church Missionary Society in Salisbury Square in London. An approach was made by them to the organisers for permission for two of their representatives to accompany the expedition. Their aim was to scout the river for sites to establish Christian missions amongst the people living on its banks. Some people in England did not support such an expedition. But, despite their misgivings, the expedition received the stamp of royal approval when no other a personage than Prince Albert, the Consort of Queen Victoria, himself attended a special service to commemorate the Europeans who were going on the expedition. As Sir Samuel Buxton, a Member of Parliament, who had succeeded William Wilberforce as leader of the Anti-Slavery movement, and one of the sponsors of the expedition remarked, *'the sum total of what was needed for the benefit of Africa was the Gospel and the plough.'* In other words, Christianity and industry.

As the ships were to call at Freetown to take on supplies, the Church Missionary Society in London, decided that while the ships were in Freetown, Adjai , who was about 32 at the time and by then a young catechist at the Fourah Bay Institute, was to join them to help bring the gospel to the heathens they might encounter. Also to join the expedition was the Reverend James Frederick Schon, a German, who had spent ten years in Sierra Leone as a missionary, and was an authority on the Africans and their characteristics. Schon who was born in 1803, was trained at the Basel Missionary Seminary, and at the Church Missionary Society

Training College at Islington in London, where he was ordained in 1832 and sent to Sierra Leone. He served in various parishes in the Colony for over six years, before returning to England. He married three times. He and Adjai were to join the expedition to represent the CMS, and although both men were keen to go on the expedition, their wives had their doubts, especially as it would mean perhaps years of separation, with very little or no means of communication.

Also was the fact that Mrs. Schon was recovering from a serious illness, and her husband was reluctant to leave her alone. For Adjai ,the parting was also not easy. Apart from leaving behind his wife and family, he was also reluctant to be parted from his beloved Fourah Bay Institute and his work there. But, true to their faith and long series of prayers for God's guidance, both Schon and Adjai convinced their wives that what they were doing was the Lords work, as they left for the unknown. Rather reluctantly both wives agreed to them going on the expedition. They took with them twelve interpreters selected from amongst the ex-slaves in Freetown, who spoke Hausa, Ibo, Kakanda, Yoruba, Bornou, Nufi Benin, Filatah and Eggara.

We are lucky today, that both these men kept copious notes and left extensive journals for us to read about what happened during the journey. Adjai writes:

'1 July.

This morning I took my boxes on board the 'Soudan' Mrs Crowther and several of my friends accompanying me. I afterward returned on shore to spend the remainder of the day with them, as the vessel was not to get under weigh until that evening. At about 5 0'clock I took an affectionate leave of my wife, children and friends. In the vessel I was placed in the engineers' mess. At about 11 o'clock the Soudan got under weigh for the Niger, the highway into the heart of Africa. She was soon followed by the Wilberforce, which took her in tow in order to save fuel. When I look back on the colony in which I have spent nineteen years - the happiest part of my life, because there I made acquaintance with the saving knowledge of Jesus Christ - leaving my wife who was near her confinement, and four children behind - I could not but feel pain and some anxiety for a time at the separation. May the Lord, who has been my guide from my youth up until now, keep them and me, and make me neither barren nor unfruitful in His service.'

Adjai was disappointed that he and Schon were not to travel on the same ship. He on the 'Soudan' and Schon on the Wilberforce. He would have liked them to be together so they could work jointly in their leisure time translating the Scriptures into one or two of the languages. But, alas, it was not to happen and one can today wonder whether this separation was not the beginning of the racism that was to bug him in later years.

The first port of call was at Cape Coast where Adjai went ashore to look for the grave of Rev. Philip Quaque, an African who some ninety years earlier had been sent to Britain as a young man by the Society for the Propagation of the Gospel in 1754, and had been baptised at St. Mary's, in Islington on 7 January, 1759. He returned as a fully ordained priest to his homeland, to work and spread the Gospel of God for more than fifty years. He died in 1816. Adjai must have wondered that although he was a teacher/worker for Christianity, when would he be called to become a priest? He did not know then what God had ordained for him by the time the expedition ended.

The first part of the expedition went without any mishap, and soon they were steaming up the river Niger. The captains made contact with the chiefs they came across, and observed that the prospects of trade with good profits could be made. At Aboh they met with King Obi, one of the most important local rulers, who was impressed with them, and after days of discussions, signed an agreement to abolish the slave trade. Rev. Schon, who had arranged the treaty with him described the meeting with the King, a man of average size with a pleasant smile. *'King Obi sent one of his sons to welcome the strangers. He was a very fine-looking young man, about twenty years of age. Both himself and his companions attended our morning devotion, after which I told them what book it was of which I had been reading a portion, and that I had come to this country to tell the people what God had in it revealed to us. They were surprised, and could not well understand how it was possible that I should have no other object in view. They are sensible of their inferiority in every respect to white men and can therefore be easily led by them either to do evil, or good.*

When I told one this morning that the slave trade was a bad thing, and that white people wished to put an end to it altogether, he gave me an excellent answer, 'Well, if white people give up buying, black people will give up selling slaves'. He assured me too, that it had hitherto been his belief, that it was the will of God that black people should be slaves of white people.

This afternoon I satisfied myself of the correctness of various particulars which I had previously obtained of the Ibo people respecting some of their superstitious practices. It appears to be but too true that human sacrifices are offered by them and that in the most barbarous manner.'

After the meeting with King Obi, the expedition went on its merry way up the river. But, what it did not realise was that the Europeans on board, were not used to the climate, and their numbers were decimated by the disease malaria, which at that time, was not known that it was carried by mosquitoes. One after another they fell ill with the fever and died, causing great distress on all the ships. Even Rev. Shon became ill, but luckily survived. But, for some reason, due perhaps to his immunity, Adjai remained well and had to pray with, and comfort those who fell ill. A great loss was their Ingalla interpreter, whom they had come to rely on. He fell overboard and drowned in the fast flowing river. All these deaths did cast a gloom on the expedition. At one stage the ships were so full of the sick, that it was decided that two ships, the *Wilberforce* and the *Soudan*, were to carry the invalids back to sea, away from the river with its infestations and death. Adjai was very happy with this as it gave him the opportunity of joining Rev. Schon in his ship, so that they could work together.

But in spite of all this, Captain Trotter of the *Albert* moved the ships up the river, and they put in at a place called Gori where Adjai used his language skill to negotiate with the chief. The chief, who was about seventy years old, did not speak but had a mouthpiece or speaker, who did the interpreting for him. He denied any knowledge of the number of slaves brought to his territory, or if they were the subjects of the neighbouring chief. Their next stop was at Egga where, after a long wait of about an hour outside the palace of chief Rogang, he appeared. Adjai recorded that he then informed the chief about the reason for the visit, saying **that '*the Queen of the country called Great Britain, has sent the king of the ship to all the chiefs of Africa to make treaties with them to give up war and the slave trade - to all their people in the cultivation of the soil, and to mind all that white people say to them, as they wish to teach them many things and particularly the Book, which God gives, which will make all men happy. I added likewise that there are many Nufi, Hausa and Yoruba people in the white man's country who have been liberated from the Portuguese and Spanish slave ships, that they are now living like white men, and they pray to God and learn his Book, and consequently they are living a happier*** *life than they were in their own country, and much better of than their country people are at present. To this many of them said that they could judge of their happy state merely by my appearance. I added moreover, that our country people in the white man's country had written a letter to the Queen who lives in Great Britain, expressing their wish to return to their country, if she would send white men to accompany them. But, the Queen who loves us all as her children, told them to stop until she had first sent ships to all the chiefs of Africa to persuade them to give up wars and the slave trade, and if they consented to her proposals she would gladly grant the request of our country people.'*

The chief listened intently to what Adjai said, but he then informed him that he could do nothing unless he consulted with the King of Rabba, under whom he owed his authority. But Adjai was able to obtain some useful information from chief Rogang. This included the fact that the population had succumbed to the evil of alcohol, which was traded amongst them.

But, this was not the worse aspect of the journey up the river Niger by the expedition. As Adjai recorded in his journal, sickness and death bugged the expedition all the way. Captain Trotter was soon laid low, as did Captain Allen, who soon died and was buried ashore. It was then left to the first mate to navigate the ship. One sailor, delirious from the fever, flung himself overboard, but luckily he was saved and brought back and tied down in his hammock. So, within a space of seven days three officers and a sailor died and were buried in unmarked graves. The banks of the river Niger are littered with the bones of the brave British men who risked their lives in the service of the Church Missionary Society, Queen Victoria and her government. The pain and suffering experienced by the people who went on the expedition was expressed by the Rev. Schon in his journal. He wrote, *'Pain of body, distress of mind, weakness, sobbing and crying on all sides. The healthy, if so they may be called, are more like walking shadows than men of enterprise. Truly Africa is an unhealthy country. When will her redemption draw nigh? All human skill is baffled, all human means falls short. Forgive us, O God, if on them we have depended and be forgetful of Thee and let the light of Thy countenance again shine upon us that we may be healed.'*

Adjai himself wrote in his journal, *'it appears as if the Niger was doomed to remain in perpetual seclusion and its mighty waters destined to float down only human cargo, aggravating the miseries of the country and her people.'*

So, it was that of one hundred and fifty Europeans who started on the expedition, forty-two died in the space of two months. When the expedition finally limped back to Fernando Po, the sick were landed and lodged in various houses in the town with the hope that with care, they would survive. However, the purser Mr Willie, Captain Allen and three officers and a marine all breathed their last. But, Adjai and many of the African who went with him, survived to tell the tale. Because of this high loss of life, the expedition had to be abandoned, without fulfilling the object for which they had set out with such high hopes, and the remnants struggled back to civilisation. But, it left a lasting impression on Adjai, whose faith in the Almighty was tested to the limit as he saw strong men, who had been his traveling companions reduced to gibbering idiots when the fever got to them, and he had to officiate at their funerals. So, although the expedition was deemed a failure, yet it did lead to a better understanding of some of the tribes on the banks of the river, and opened the way for more expeditions to come in the future. The failure came as a shock to the CMS and the government in Britain, who had wholeheartedly backed and financed it. This did put off another expedition to the river Niger for another decade to come.

CHAPTER 5
A PRIEST, AT LAST

Adjai survived, and as did the Rev. Schon, although he had been ill for some time during the expedition. He survived to help write the report about what took place, which he sent to the CMS in London. In the report the good Reverend said that after the needless waste of European life, thoughts should be given to the importance of building up the native ministries. He praised Adjai highly for his contribution to the expedition, and also recommended that he be considered for ordination to the priesthood. In his recommendation Rev. Schon wrote:

'I have thought much about the propriety of Samuel Crowther's returning to England with me and receiving ordination, and should be happy to learn what opinion the Parent Committee may form of this plan on my return to Sierra Leone. Of his decided piety I have no doubt; his studious habits and anxiety to improve himself would after a few weeks' attention, qualify him in other respects. He is highly esteemed by all who know him, and his love for his country and for his people would prevail on him to lay himself out for their good. The committee in Sierra Leone was ever in favour of this measure, and his excellent conduct in this expedition can only raise our opinion of him.'

Adjai also received another testimonial from the Rev. F. Bultimam, one of the missionaries in Sierra Leone dated 13th October,1841. He wrote:

"There is no one more fit to be entrusted with the ministry of the Gospel, among his own brethren, than Samuel Crowther. However rarely the solid knowledge of Samuel Crowther is found among his brethren; it is so far more rarely combined with such modesty as his; and I am convinced that he would do honour to our Society, if presented by them as a candidate for Holy Orders to the Bishop of London. I sincerely wish and hope that on his return from the Niger this opportunity of evincing the innate prowess of an African mind will be afforded him, though I am sure his modesty will not allow him to ask for it.'

With such recommendations, the CMS in London could do nothing but agree to the ordination of Adjai into the priesthood. So, no sooner was he returned to Freetown from the doomed expedition, and was reunited with his family than he had to be parted from them again. This time, it was for him to travel to England for his training as a priest. He left his wife and family and reached England on 3 September, 1842. Whilst he was at sea he spent the time working on the translation of the Yoruba language, preparing the grammar and vocabulary. This was in preparation for translation of the Bible into Yoruba. But, before that came about, he was to publish 'A **VOCABULARY OF THE YORUBA LANGUAGE**' while he was in England. And it can be said that his ability to speak and write the language, was to help him in his mission work to spread the Gospel amongst his people in Nigeria.

While in London, Adjai was able to convince the CMS that the expedition had not been a complete failure, as had been believed, and some good did come out of it. In London he was attached to the C.M.S. Training College, in Upper Street, Islington in North London, where he studied for his ordination as a priest. The principal of the college was the Reverend C. F. Childe. The college had been setup in 1825 to train Anglican Missionaries to serve overseas. It closed in 1915. But, when Adjai was there in 1842, he took his studies seriously and diligently, and with his nose to the grind stone, he completed the course and passed the examination with flying colours. The final examination was conducted by the Rev. John Schofield, Regius Professor of Greek at Cambridge. One of the questions in the examination he had to answer was on 'Paley's Evidence of Christianity.' The Professor was so impressed by how Adjai tackled the question that he said to the Principal of the college, *I would like, with your permission, to take young Crowthers' answers to those Paley questions back with me to Cambridge, and there read a few of them in the Combination Room to certain of my old Trinity friends. If, after hearing that young African's answers they still contend that he does not possess a logical faculty, they will tempt us to question whether they do not lack other faculties of at least equal importance, such as common fairness of judgment and Christian candour.'* High praise indeed from such an eminent personage, for such a young African only a few years away from slavery.

And so on Trinity Sunday, 11 June, 1843 he received the rite of ordination from the hands of Dr. Bloomfield, Bishop of London and was invited to breakfast at Fulham Palace. Four months later in

October, he was admitted into full Holy Orders. The ordination service took place at St Paul's Cathedral, as he became the first African to become a minister of the flock of Christ and the successful product of the Church Missionary Society. It should here be stated that the ceremony took place exactly twenty-one years, less one week, after as a little slave boy he was liberated and put ashore in Freetown by the British frigate *Myrmidon*. Dr. Bloomfield, in his sermon at the ceremony said:

'What cause of Thanksgiving to Him, who hath made of one blood all nations of men, is to be found in the thought that has not only blessed the labourer of the Society by bringing many of these neglected and persecuted people to the knowledge of a saviour, but that from among a race who were despised as being incapable of intellectual exertion and acquirement. He has raised up men well qualified, even in point of knowledge, to communicate to others the saving truth which they have themselves embraced, and to become preachers of the Gospel to their brethren according to the flesh.'

Adjai preached his first sermon as a priest at the pulpit of Northrepps Church in the presence of one of his staunch supporters, Sir Thomas Buxton. Then quite old and frail, but he rejoiced to hear one of the oppressed people he had fought for and championed all his life, now preaching the Lords' Gospel. Soon after receiving Holy Orders, Adjai was on his way back home and on 2 December, 1843, he arrived to a rousing welcome from his family, and from the Christians and the Church in Freetown.

Great was the rejoicing when he returned to Freetown. He preached his first sermon in English on the Sunday after his return, to a large crowd which filled the church. He chose as his text, appropriately enough, *'And yet there is room.'* He administered the sacrament to the large crowd of his people. That evening, when all the fuss of the welcome had died down, he wrote in his journal:

'December 3. Preached my first sermon in Africa. The novelty of seeing a native clergyman performing divine service excited a very great interest among all who were present. But, the question 'Who maketh thee to differ?' filled me with shame and confusion of face. It pleases the Disposer of all hearts to give me favour in the sight of His people, and wherever I go they welcome me as a messenger of Christ.'

Later on, he preached in his native Yoruba to the large re-captive congregation now living in Freetown. The news of the arrival in Freetown of the first native clergyman spread in the community like wild fire and hundreds of people gathered to hear him preach his first sermon in Yoruba, a language they knew well. For the next year, or so, Adjai taught and preached to the people of Freetown, holding twice weekly services, and was content to be with his ever growing family. On 24 September, 1844, his wife gave birth to a son who was named Dandeson Coates, after Dandeson Coates, one of the CMS secretaries. Another son was born on 13 September, 1850, but died two hours after he was born. This birth greatly weakened his wife even though the labour was not too prolonged. He also spent the time translating the Gospel of St. Luke, the Acts of the Apostles and the Epistle to the Romans into Yoruba. But, he was not to stay in Freetown with his family for long; soon he was on another expedition, but this time he was able to take his family with him.

CHAPTER 6
ANOTHER EXPEDITION

In the year 1829 warfare had broken out amongst the Egba people in Nigeria, after one of their chiefs had shot and killed one of the leaders of another tribe, the Ife people. The refugees from this war had then fled and reached a place with a large rock called 'Olumo.' There they had founded a town called Abeokuta, which translated means 'the town under the rock'. Their leader was called Sodeke who became their king. The town grew and prospered and became a rival to Ibadan, which was close by.

For years, several of the liberated former slaves in Freetown wanted to return to the country from whence they had been taken forcibly. In 1837, some emancipated former slaves who were from the Hausa tribe, were returning from Trinidad, on their way home to carry on the anti-slave campaign. They arrived in Freetown early in 1837 on their way to Badagry, which then was a slave transit port. Naturally, they attracted a great deal of attention amongst the re-captives who had been petitioning the authorities for some time now, to allow them to return back to where they had come from originally. Spurred on by the arrival of the Hausa former slaves, they clubbed together with the Hausas' to buy a ship, which they called *Queen Victoria* after the queen in England. They bought goods with which to trade, and took on some sixty-seven passengers. These sixty-seven were selected from the over two hundred who had applied. They petitioned that a missionary accompany them, to which the CMS agreed and accordingly they found their way to Abeokuta, where they were restored to their kinfolk. Their kinfolk were amazed at their survival, as they recounted how they had been liberated by the English who had protected them, and how they had come to receive and be baptised into Christianity.

At that time the CMS was not as yet looking to get a foothold in other parts of West Africa. But having established themselves in Freetown, their next port for bringing the gospel and enlightenment was Nigeria, which was still the main country for the capturing and sale of slaves. So it was they decided that feelers should be put out to find out how they would be accepted in that country. They chose Abeokuta, where the group of recaptives had settled. The person they chose to make the visit was one Henry Townsend, an English catechist in Freetown. The twenty-one year old frail-looking missionary, was accompanied by a Yoruba speaking Sierra Leonean by the name of Andrew Wilhelm. The sponsor of the trip was a Sierra Leonean, Captain Harry Johnson, who traded regularly between Freetown and Badagry. He gave Townsend, Wilhelm and fifty other recaptives who wanted to return home, free passage on his ship the *Wilberforce*. The trip was one of reconnaissance and exploratory to find out the prospect of the CMS establishing a mission in Abeukuta, which was one of the largest towns in Yoruba land.

They reached Abeokuta on 4 January, 1843 and were very well received by the Alake, or King called Sodeke, the chiefs and the people. Sodeke was very pleased to receive Townsend and entreated him that they would welcome a missionary who might come and dwell amongst them. Townsend did not commit the CMS fully to the establishment of a mission in Abeokuta, but told the Alake that he would return after consulting his superiors in London. Townsend left Andrew Wilhelm in Abeokuta and returned to Freetown with the good news. Soon he was recalled to England with the report of his visit, and to be ordained as a priest.

When Townsend returned to Freetown, he brought a letter to Adjai from the CMS in London, asking whether he would be prepared to go on an expedition to Abeokuta in Nigeria, together with Townsend and a German missionary, Herr Gollmer. His wife was not too keen on being separated from Adjai yet again, nor was he keen to be separated from Susan and the children. In fact it had been decided in London that he would be accompanied by his wife and children, as would the Gollmer and Townsend families. The news of the expedition was well received in Freetown and Sir William Ferguson the Governor, (1842-1848) was especially pleased and sympathetic about the expedition. The people were also pleased and offers of help and money flowed in from them. On the morning that they set of, the Governor invited all the missionaries to have breakfast with him at Government House at the end of which, prayers were said for the success of the expedition; finally, the hymn, **'Guide me, O thou great Redeemer'** was sung.

The party that sailed that day on 18 December, 1844, consisted of Reverend & Mrs Townsend, Mr & Mrs Gollmer, the Europeans, the Rev.

& Mrs Crowther and their two little children, Juliana and Dandeson. Also in the party was a Mr. Marsh, a catechist and his wife and two children; a Mr. Phillips, a schoolmaster; Mr. Mark Willoughby, the interpreter, his wife and three children. In the party also were four carpenters, one being Mr. Puddicombe, three labourers and two native servants. Mr. Willoughby had been liberated at the same time as Mrs. Crowther. They had all been taught at the same time in Bathurst to write, and read the Word of God, by Mrs Weekes.

They reached Monrovia on Christmas day, their first port of call, and later anchored in Badagry, Nigeria on 17 January, 1845. This date can be said to be the start of the Church Missionary Society Christian mission in Nigeria.

The party was hoping to go straight away to Abeokuta as soon as they set foot on Nigerian soil. As it was the dry season, it would be easier to travel by foot overland. But, this did not happen. They were held up in Badagry for the next eighteen months. The reason for this delay was that by the time the party reached Badagry, they received news that the leader of the people in Abeokuta, the Alake Shodeke, who had agreed with Townsend to open a mission there, had died. His successor, Segbua, was torn between having the missionaries set up the mission in the town on the one hand and the entreaties of the Muslim Fulani slave traders, who found their infamous trade depleted with the arrival of the Christian missionaries, on the other. A notorious slave trader by the name of Domingo, was offering the new leader large sums of money, and offering to clear the roads of robbers, if he would let him carry on his dastardly trade. This must have been tempting to the new chief, the Alake but, eventually the missionaries were able to persuade him through their emissary that they were anxious to come to begin their work and he eventually agreed.

Adjai, Townsend and Herr Gollmer had not been idle during the eighteen months delay. They decided to set up a small mission in Badagry. At first they held services under a large tree in the market place, and Adjai preached in Yoruba, which at first attracted a small crowd. But, the congregation soon grew to outstrip the space under the tree. So, they decided to build a church where worship could take place and so, on 2 March, 1845 the new church with a school attached opened for business as the first Christian church and school to be erected in Nigeria. The school was soon attracting over forty children each week, and as Adjai wrote in his diary on 13 April, 1845 **'The children seemed to be particularly delighted with the service and were heard distinctly joining in the Confession, the Lord's Prayer, the Creed and the Responses to the Ten Commandments in the Yoruba language.'**

Soon, the missionaries opened a Sunday School which was regularly attended by a large number of children. And so as 1845 ended and 1846 arrived Adjai, Townsend and Gollmer continued to minister to their growing flock. During their enforced stay in Badagry, Adjai took the opportunity to progress with the translation of the Scriptures and the Liturgy into the Yoruba language. Townsend also took the opportunity of trying to become perfect in the Yoruba tongue.

In July 1846, they received word that permission had been granted by chief Segbua the Alake that they were to travel to Abeokuta. And so with great rejoicing on the 27th, the party was finally on its way to the promised land of Abeokuta. But, sadly they had to leave Mr Gollmer behind to take care of the mission and church. His beloved wife had died and was buried in the churchyard. Describing the sad demise of Mrs Gollmer, Adjai wrote, *'This is the first Christian funeral that has ever been performed in this country. Many of the natives, out of curiosity, accompanied us to the church and to the burial ground to witness the burial of a Christian. Though our dear sister is dead, yet she speaks to the natives around, and shows the difference between death of a saint and the death of a heathen. The scene of this day will not be soon wear away from the minds of those who were present - about 150 persons. The chiefs having been informed of our mournful bereavement, send their messengers to express their sympathy with us. Although no worshipers of the great God who made all things, yet they invariably ascribed this afflictive visitation to the province of God, who knew and ordered all the events of life in His secret wisdom. Truly, although they knew Him as God, "they glorify Him not as God," but became vain in their imaginations and their foolish hearts are darkened.'*

But, the journey to Abeokuta was not easy, or uneventful. They were beset with storms and driving rain and had only inadequate cover for such a large party. The going was tough on all of them, but especially on Mrs. Crowther, who after being tipped over from her hammock several times, practically entered Abeokuta on foot. By then she was extremely tired. The two children, Juliana and Dandeson, fared better as they were carried African style on the backs of the bearers all the way. Their progress was very slow, and they had to be on the alert for wild animals and the fear of being attacked by unfriendly native villagers, not least by marauding slavers. But despite such hardships, they were protected by their Christian faith and they reached the city on 3 August, 1846. There they received a great welcome from King Segbua, who had sent guides to help bring them safely to their final destination. They were glad to be reunited with Andrew Wilhelm who had held the fort since Townsend left. During this period the community from Sierra Leone had been administered to by Wilhelm and by their own evangelism. The following day Adjai addressed the Alake and the whole town in Yoruba, and told them about the mission he was going to set up, about the Christian God and the blessings that he would bring to the nation. The Alake thanked him for coming to Abeokuta, gave him land on which to build the church, and offered his people to help with the work. Adjai was delighted with the offer and soon the first mission church in Abeokuta was completed. This was funded partly by a donation of twenty-six pounds from the recaptives in Freetown and forty pounds from friends in England.

The mission then set about the training of young men in building, printing and in medicine, and setup apprenticeship schemes for the cotton trade. It not only had a Yoruba speaking priest but also a printed study of the language that Townsend had published and brought with him. During the years 1847 to 1850, Adjai was busy in writing or translating several books into Yoruba. He wrote and published a Yoruba Schools Prima in 1849, which was reprinted in 1852 and 1853. He worked on the translations of the Gospel into Yoruba, and between 1850 and 1856 he annually published at least one book of the Old or New Testament. And in 1850 he completed and published part of the Anglican Prayer Book in Yoruba. Although a fire destroyed much of his work on the translation of the bible into Yoruba, yet he persevered and in the 1880s, a few years before his death, the work was completed and the Bible in Yoruba was published. The greatest testament to his service to his Lord.

But that was not all, for it looks as if the God who had saved Adjai from slavery had now guided him to this place of Abeokuta. For only after being there for three weeks, that it was here that Adjai received one of the greatest gift any man can hope for. A meeting with his long lost mother. The meeting is here recorded by Adjai himself in his diary:

'August 21. The text for this day in the Christian Almanac, is "Thou art the Helper of the fatherless." I never felt the force of this text more than I did this day, as I have to relate that

my mother, from whom I was torn away about five-and-twenty years ago, came with my brother in quest of me. When she saw me, she trembled. She could not believe her eyes. We grasped one another, looking at each other with silence and great astonishment, big tears rolling down her emaciated cheeks. A great number of people soon came together. She trembled as she held me by the hand and called me by the familiar names by which I well remember I used to be called by my grandmother, who has since died in slavery. We could not say much, but sat still and cast now and then an affectionate look at each other - a look which violence and oppression had long checked - an affection which had nearly been extinguished by the long space of twenty-five years. My two sisters who had been captured with us are both with my mother, who takes care of them and her grandchildren in a small town not far from here, called Abaka. Thus, unsort for - after all search for me had failed - God has brought us together again, and turned our sorrow into joy.'

THE MOTHER OF BISHOP SAMUEL ADJAI CROWTHER

The story Alafa had to tell her son was one of violence and savagery. Soon after being parted from him in Dah'dah, she was able to escape from the man who had purchased her. His sister remained in slavery as, she Alafa had no money to redeem her. But later she was able to borrow about six pounds in the local currency to redeem her daughter from her master, who was very cruel to her. They had made inquiries about the whereabouts of Adjai, but nothing was heard about him. After two years of searching they gave him up as lost forever. But many years afterward, when she was living with her daughters and grand-children in Abaka, on her way to a neighbouring market-town with her eldest daughter Lanre, who was married and had a month old baby, they were captured by slavers, and once again separated.

Eventually her daughter and child were redeemed by her husband, but she, Alafa, was taken from place to place. They tried to sell her but, as she was then too old, no one would purchase her. She became a sort of housekeeper, and one day on her way to the market to purchase food for her mistress, she was again captured by some people and brought to Abeokuta. She was in bondage there for five years, until her daughters could redeem her. Since then, she has been living in Abaka taking care of her grandchildren. And it was while there that she heard about this new preacher who was preaching about this new God, in their own language. And it was this new God which guided her footsteps to this place where she found that the preacher was her long lost son, Adjai.

She left her daughters Lanre and Amosa and their husbands and children in Abaka, and came to live with Adjai and his family in Abeokuta. And on 5 February, 1848, she was baptised by her son at the Abeokuta Mission Church and given the name Hannah. The name had been chosen carefully by Adjai; for the biblical Hannah had no greater reason to rejoice in her Samuel, than this African Hannah had in her Samuel. Despite all the hardships she had endured all her life, she lived until she died aged 97 years in Lagos on 13 October, 1883.

Soon after mother and son were reunited, war broke out between Abeokuta and Abaka, and the family of Adjai were captured and brought to Abeokuta as slaves. These were his two sisters Lanre and Amosa, one of their husbands and several nephews and nieces. The husband of one sister

Amosa, had been ill when captured and had been left to die in the bush on the way to Abeokuta. Adjai, with the help of some of the people he had converted, was able to ransom them from slavery. So once again the family was reunited and they all lived happily with Adjai in Abeokuta.

The mission prospered and in his diary on 3 August, 1849, Adjai wrote: *'This mission today is three years old. What has God wrought during this short interval of conflict light and darkness? We have 500 constant attendants on the means of grace, about 80 communicants and nearly 200 candidates for baptism. A great number of heathens have ceased worshipping their country's gods; others have cast theirs away altogether, and are not far from enlisting under the banner of Christ.'*

When Townsend was recalled to London because of the illness of his wife and for consultations about the progress of the mission, the Alake and other chiefs, without any prompting, sent him with a letter to the Queen with their expression of gratitude for bringing Christianity to them and for suppressing the slave trade. They also urged that trade and commerce should be continued. In the letter they wrote, *'We have seen your servants the missionaries; what they have done is agreeable to us. They have built a house of God. They have taught the people the Word of God and our children beside. We begin to understand them.'*

When the letter was received by the CMS and the government in London, the government instructed the Earl of Chichester to reply to the letter. This he did, and when the reply reached Abeokuta, Adjai gathered all the various chiefs together on 23 May, 1849 and read them the reply, translating the letter word for word. In part the letter said: *'The Queen and people of Great Britain are very glad to know that Segbua and the chiefs think as they do upon the subject of commerce. But commerce alone will not make a nation great and happy like England. England has been great and happy by the knowledge of the true God and Jesus Christ. The Queen is, therefore very glad to hear that Segbua and the chiefs have so kindly received the missionaries who carry with them the Word of God and that so many people are willing to hear it.'*

Accompanying the letter were presents of two Bibles, one in English and the other in Arabic, from the Queen. From Prince Albert came a steel corn mill, which put the people in awe when it was first used.

The work of the mission was much expanded with the arrival of the Reverend D. Hilderer, and the Rev. J. C. Muller, both of whom proved very valuable helpers to Adjai. The work of the Mission was attracting great interest in England, and money and gifts were regularly sent by people interested in the Christian work that was being done in the name of God in this land that was then considered to be *'darkest and heathen'* Africa. Children also sent toys and books, some addressed especially to the children of Adjai and Mrs. Crowther. Here is the reply to a girl in England, who had sent some books to the

Crowther children, Julianna and Dandeson. Dated 11 June,1849 from Abeokuta, and signed by Julianna, but in her father's handwriting:

"My dear Ellen,

My papa read your kind letter to me and Dandeson, and gave us the little books which you denied yourself the pleasure of sweet sugar plums in order to purchase for us. We like them very much, and as we cannot understand all that they contain yet, our papa has kept them in good order for us till we can read them through and understand all in them. He carefully put them up in envelopes, but we like now and then to look at them and return them to him for safe keeping. I remember the time when we were crossing the river on the backs of our carriers, but Dandeson, being much younger, almost forgets all about it: the journey of four days in the bush on the backs of men was very tiresome. I have seen the picture of our crossing that river called Mojuba.

My papa has a great deal to do. As I cannot write a good letter yet, he has kindly done it for me. I am learning to write in copy-books which papa gave me, and I hope to be able to write myself, as my elder sister, who is now in England, can do. Miss Lanfear saw her. My mama teaches me to sew and to mark canvas and I shall soon be able to master all my letters. I have some native school companions living with mama; they knew not a letter when they first came, and did not know how to hold needles, but since mama has taken pains with them they can now hem and make stitches and they learn to read and very fast in school. Four of them have been baptised by papa at the earnest request of their their parents.

I hope you will pray for us all that we may grow up good children and love the Lord Jesus Christ from our childhood.

My mama desires her kind love to you and your kind aunt, who wrote your letter.

Dandeson has gone to bed, but I am sure he would also send his love to you. Our grandmama is quite well; she has been baptised. I remain, Yours affectionately Julianna Crowther."

In August 1851, Adjai was invited to London by no more an eminent a personage than the Foreign Secretary, Lord Palmerston, who was anxious to learn more about the mission in Abeokuta. Adjai travelled with his wife and two children, Julianna and Dandeson. This visit gave him the opportunity to discuss his Christian work with all the most important persons in the Government, including the Prime Minister Lord John Russell, and with no less a personage than Queen Victoria and Prince Albert. At a meeting with Lord Palmerstone, Adjai gave him a short history of the political situation in West Africa, with especial emphasis on what was happening in Abeokuta. He also touched on the slave trade, which unfortunately was still going on in Dahomey, which was not only hampering commerce and trade, but also the work of the Christian mission. Before returning home, Adjai received a letter from Lord Palmerston, in which he expressed his pleasure at the interview with him, and added:

'I am glad to have had an opportunity of thanking you again for the important and interesting information with regard to Abeokuta which you communicated to me when I had the pleasure of seeing you at my house in August last year. Request that you will assure your countrymen that Her Majesty's Government take a lively interest in the welfare of the Egba nation and of the community settled at Abeokuta, which town seems to be a centre from which the lights of Christianity and of civilisation may be spread over the neighbouring country.'

On the 18 November, accompanied by the Prime Minister, Adjai travelled to Windsor Castle, where he was kindly received by the Prince Consort, where they discussed the position of the affairs in West Africa. It was then that he met Queen Victoria for the first time.

My grandmother used to tell us about how her grandfather Adjai, would regale she, her brothers, sisters and cousins, all his grandchildren, and with much laughter, and a twinkle in his eyes, about his coming face to face with Queen Victoria. This is how Adjai recorded the visit many years later:

'Through the kind recommendation of the then Hon. Secretary of the CMS, the late Rev.Henry Venn, on the slave trade question agitating the minds of the Members of Parliament at the time, on 18 November, 1851 at 4.30.pm, Lord Wriothesley Russell kindly took me to the Palace of Windsor. On arrival there Prince Albert was not in; the Servant-in-Waiting went to seek him. While we were waiting in a drawing-room I

could not help looking around at the magnificence of the room glittering with gold, the carpet and chairs, all brilliant. While in this state of mind the door was opened, and I saw a lady gorgeously dressed, with a long train, step gracefully in. I thought she was the Queen. I rose at once, and was ready to kneel and pay obeisance, but she simply bowed to us, said not a word, took something from the mantelpiece and retired. After she left Lord Russell told me she was one of the Ladies-in-Waiting. 'Well,' I said to myself, 'if a Lady-in-Waiting is so superbly dressed, what will be that of the Queen herself!'

Soon, we were invited to an upper drawing-room, more richly furnished than the first. Here, we met Prince Albert standing by a writing-table. Lord Russell made obeisance and introduced me, and I made obeisance. A few words of introductory remarks led to conversation about West Africa in general, and Abeokuta in particular. The Prince asked whether we could find the place on any map, or thereabout. I then showed the position in the large map from the Blue Book, and brought from my pocket the small one, which Adjai's son, Samuel had made on the section of the slave trade influence, with the different towns and seaports legibly shown. About this time a lady came in, simply dressed and the Prince, looking behind him, introduced her to Lord Russell, but in so quick a way that I could not catch the sound. This lady and the Prince turned towards the map to find Abeokuta and Sierra Leone, where the slaves are liberated. All the time I was in blissful *ignorance of the Great Majesty before whom I stood and was conversing freely and answering every question put to me about the way slaves are entrapped in their homes, or caught as captives in war. On inquiry I gave them the history of how I was caught and sold, to which all of them listened with breathless attention. It was getting dusk, a lamp was got, and the Prince was anxious to find and define the relative positions of the different places on the map, especially Lagos, which was the principle seaport from which Yoruba slaves were shipped; and when the Prince wanted to* open the Blue Book map wider, it blew the lamp out altogether and there was a burst of laughter from the Prince, the lady and from Lord Russell. The Prince then said 'Will your Majesty kindly bring us a candle from the mantelpiece?' On hearing this I became aware of the person before whom I was all the time. I trembled from head to foot, and could not open my mouth to answer the question that followed.

QUEEN VICTORIA AND PRINCE ALBERT
WHOM ADJAI MET AT WINDSOR CASTLE

Lord Russell and the Prince told me not to be frightened, and the smiles on the face of the good Queen assured me that she was not angry at the liberty I had taken speaking so freely before her, and so my fears subsided. I pointed out Lagos, the particular object of the inquiry, and told them that I and others were shipped from that place and showed the facility which that port has, beyond all other ports, as a depot, being much nearer, and the port of the highway to the interior Yoruba countries. The Prince said, 'Lagos must be knocked down, by all means; as long as they have the lake (lagoon) to screen themselves, and the Men-of-War outside, it is of no use.'

'The Queen was highly please to hear this. Lord Russell then mentioned my translations into the Yoruba language of the Gospel and I repeated, by request, the Lords Prayer in Yoruba, which the Queen said was a soft and melodious language. Lord Russell informed the Queen of my having seen Sir H. Leeke, who rescued me and others from the slave ship many years ago, which interested her very much. She was told that Mrs Crowther was rescued in the same way that I was, and she asked whether she was in England, and was told so. She asked after Sally Forbes Bonetta, the Yoruba African young girl rescued from Dahomey. After these questions she withdrew with a marked farewell gesture.

The meeting was also recorded briefly in the diary of Queen Victoria when on 18 November, 1851, she wrote *'On coming home, I saw in Albert's room, an African missionary M Crowther, who was brought by L. Wriothersley Russell. M Crowther was ordained a few years ago.'*

The Yoruba African young girl referred to by the Queen, was Sally Forbes Bonetta, who was the adopted daughter of the Queen. Her story is also as interesting as that of Adjai as they later became intertwined. I digress to tell her story here.

In May 1850, Queen Victoria sent a emissary in the person of one Captain Frederick Forbes, who was part of the West African Squadron, to King Gezo of Dahomey, known now as the Republic of Benin, to implore him to put an end to the slave trade. The Commander wrote a lengthy account about his meeting with the King in his book - **'Six months'**

Service in the African Blockage,' published in 1849. He met the King, gave him the message from the Great Queen and offered the gifts of silks and cloths the Queen she had sent him. According to the account of the meeting by Forbes himself, he and his entourage passed through several rooms and squares of the palace and saw the recently decapitated human heads, still dripping with blood.

The king listened to what Commander Forbes had to say, but gave no clue as to whether he would agree to the Queen's request. But, in return sent the Queen a present. Just before the Commander met the king, a slave raiding party had just returned with some slaves they had captured. Amongst them was a little girl aged about five or six years, whom the king plucked and handed over to the Commander as a present to Queen Victoria. Some researchers have said that she came from a village in Okeadan, which had been raided by Dahomean slave raiders, who had killed her parents when she was about five. Commander Forbes could do nothing but accept the present, who on the way back to England he named Sally after his mother, Forbes after himself and Bonetta after the name of his ship. This is how Queen Victoria described in her journal on 9 November, 1850, meeting with Sally for the first time:

'We came home, found Albert still there, waiting for Capt. Forbes & a poor little negro, girl, whom he brought back from the King of Dohemey, her parents and all her relatives having been sacrificed. Capt. Forbes saved her life, by asking for her as a present. She is 7 years old,

sharp and intelligent, & speaks English. She is dressed as any other girl. When her bonnet was taken off, her little black wooly head and big earrings gave her the true negro type.'

SALLY FORBES BONNETTA

The girl was adopted by the Queen, and her life was transformed for ever. She sent her to the Female Institution in Freetown, later to become the Annie Walsh Memorial School, under the formidable Miss Sass. The Queen was concerned that the British climate was not suitable for a young Africa girl. So, a letter from Windsor Castle to the Reverend Henry Venn, Secretary of the Church Missionary Society (CMS) formally recognising Sally as her adopted daughter stated, **'The Queen has under her protection a little African girl, about 8 years old** who was brought to this country by Commander Forbes from the King of Dahomey. The Queen having made enquiries, has been informed that the climate of this country is often fatally, hurtful to the health African children and is, therefore, anxious that this child should be educated in one of Her Majesty's dependence upon the Coast of Africa. The cost of her education was to be met by the Queen.'

In her diary dated December 1855, the Queen wrote, *'I saw Sally Forbes, the African girl who I have had educated. She is immensely grown up and has a lovely slim figure.'* Sally later married a Mr. James Pinson Labula Davies, a widower who was born in Nigeria but lived in England where he was in business. His parents had been one of the Yoruba Recaptives, who had settled in Freetown where he was educated at the CMS Grammar school in Freetown. He joined the Royal Navy, which was part of the West African Squadron. He was the son of Nigerian parents who who had become wealthy due to the palm oil trade, buying former slave ships cheaply and traded between Lagos, Badagry, Freetown and Liverpool. He was a member of the Saro community based in Lagos who contributed the funds for the Rev. T. B. Macauley, the son-in-law of Bishop Crowther to establish the Church Missionary Society Grammar School in Lagos. He also was a farmer with a farm at Ijon, just outside Lagos, where it is said he was the person who first planted cocoa in West Africa, having obtaining the seeds from a Brazilian ship and also from Fernando Po in 1879 and 1880.

Sally did not want to marry someone she did not love and who was much older than her. But Queen Victoria had strong views about a woman getting married and settling down. Finally, very reluctantly, but with the blessings of the Queen (who provided the trousseau) Sally got married in a lavish ceremony at St. Nicholas church in Brighton. The local newspaper headlined the wedding An interesting wedding. It is interesting to note that one of the officiating clergy at the wedding was the Rev. George Crowther-Nicol, the son-in-law of Adjai. The Rev. Henry Venn, Secretary of the Church Missionary Society, gave a speech in which he gave a background of Sally, and for the first time, her full names were recorded in the marriage certificate as her full names as Ina Sally Forbes Bonetta, with the space for the names for the brides' parents given as unknown. In place of their abode Sally is described a Negress of Dahomey, West Africa. The marriage certificate also gives her full names as Ina Sally Forbes Bonetta. Ina is her African name, which in Yoruba means, **Child born with the umbilical cord round her neck.**

SALLY FORBES BONNETTA AND HER
HUSBAND JAMES DAVIES

Sally, now Mrs. Davies, a married woman, first went to live in Freetown, where her husband carried on with his business whilst she took up a teaching post at her old school, the Female Institution, where she had received her early education. It was thought that at some stage Sally would head the institution, but she soon became pregnant, which ruled her out. When her daughter was born in 1863, she sought permission from the Queen to name her Victoria. The Queen agreed and became the child's Godmother. The silver salver and christening cup the Queen sent to her African God daughter, is still in the family today. The heirloom bears the inscription -

To Victoria Davies, from her Godmother Victoria,
Queen of Great Britain and Ireland.

It was made by Garrard's, the Royal silversmiths. They went on to have two more children; Arthur born in 1871 and Stella born in 1873.

Sally and her husband and child later moved to Lagos. Victoria was brought to England and Queen Victoria paid for her education at Cheltenham Ladies College. She did return to Lagos and married the successful Lagos doctor John K. Randle of a prominent Lagos family. Many of her relatives still live in Lagos, while a separate branch live in Freetown. Although Victoria did not attend the Annie Walsh Memorial School herself, yet her daughter Beatrice did. In the archive at Windsor Castle I found a letter from Sir Fleetwood Edward, Keeper of The Privy Purse from Balmoral, dated September 1900, a year before Queen Victoria died. It was addressed to the Right Rev. Taylor-Smith, Bishop of Sierra Leone and reads:

'Dear Bishop,

I believe you were kind enough at the request of Princess Henry of Battenburg to arrange for the education of Beatrice Randle at the Annie Walsh School in Freetown, at the cost of £35 a year, which the Queen has agreed to pay. I write to ask you to be good enough to advice me as to the how, as Keeper of the Privy Purse, I had better make the payment. May it be through you and how shall I remit it?'

This shows that until she died Queen Victoria did not forget her adopted African daughter and her descendants. It is interesting to note that the daughter of Beatrice, also named Sally, married Herbert Macauley, the grandson of Bishop Samuel Adjai Crowther. So, the family of two former slave children became intertwined later on in life.

Sadly, Sally died of tuberculosis in August 1880 in Madeira while on her way to England and was buried in the English Cemetery in Funchal. Her husband erected a granite obelisk-shaped monument more than eight feet high in her memory in his cocoa farm in Ijon, with this inscription:

'IN MEMORY OF PRINCESS SALLY FORBES BONNETTA, WIFE OF THE HON. J. P. L. DAVIES WHO DEPARTED THIS LIFE AT MADEIRA AUGUST 15TH 1880. AGED 37 YEARS.'

Sally's grave is numbered 206 in the British Cemetery in Funchal, situated near the Anglican Holy Trinity Church, Rua Quebra Costas Funchal, Madeira. It is now quite neglected and, sadly, there is no headstone.

The last mention of Sally in Queen Victoria's diary was that year when she wrote, **'After luncheon, saw poor Victoria Davies, my African godchild, now 17, who heard this morning of the death of her dear mother at Madeira. She came to see me, her young brother and little sister only five were with their mother. I shall give her an** annuity.' And she did so, until she died. Sally's children were educated in England paid for by the kindness of the Queen and her godchild Victoria visited her throughout her life until Queen Victoria died in 1901. In fact, Victoria Davies was one of her last visitors at Osborne House in the Isle of Wight where she died.

Back to Adjai. During this visit to England when he met Queen Victoria, Adjai had the honour of being invited as guest of the students of Cambridge University, where he gave a talk about his missionary work in West Africa. He invited them to think about coming to join him to carry on his missionary work in West Africa. In his closing remarks to the students he said, '**St Paul saw in a vision a man of Macedonia who prayed him to come over to his assistance. But, it is no vision you see now; it is a real man of Africa that stands before you, and on behalf of his countrymen invites you to come over into Africa and help us.**'

Before they returned to West Africa, a farewell meeting organised by the CMS, was held in the Parochial schoolroom in Church Street in Islington, for Adjai, his wife Asano and another missionary who would be returning with them. The good and great of the Church Missionary Society, including the president, the Earl of Leicester and the Reverend Henry Venn, the secretary of the society attended. During the speeches, praise was heaped on Adjai for the work he was doing in raising the profile of the society in West Africa and in bringing the word of God to heathen parts of the continent. The Rev Venn, speaking on behalf of the CMS, thanked God for all that he had done since the Yoruba mission had been established eight years earlier, and congratulated him for his tact in dealing with the chiefs and urged him to be careful in dealing with the slave traders. Being a far sighted man, Rev. Venn warned that the future character of the Christian Church in West Africa was at stake, and predicted that the policies and individual actions of the CMS would influence it. He went on to warn that the society's sphere of labour was different from India and New Zealand. But, here on the Niger they would have not only to spread **'Christianity, but also fix its character, organise a native church, create a Christian literature and lay plans for the future to come.'** He urged the society to aim at self government and becoming self supporting, to put the Bible in the hands of the people and said how much they were indebted to Adjai for his translation of a great portion into Yoruba of the Holy Scriptures and the Liturgy.

Then turning to Mrs Crowther, he told her how heartily England had welcomed her as the helpmate of her husband and how important they all felt her position was as the first Christian mother in Abeokuta and they rejoiced that her own children were an example to others. He then went on to bless her with these words, **'May she return with double blessing to her country-women. May she indeed be a mother to that spiritual Israel in the wilderness of Africa. May the native church, once confined to the house of Samuel Crowther, become a national church, but still retaining its character as an aggregation of Christian households bound together by one common tie of** love and union with Christ, in whom all the families of the earth are blessed.'

In reply Adjai also spoke about the time when Africans would be able to run the affairs of the church themselves in West Africa. **'These native Christians are quite ready with reason for the truth as it is in them, and can stand their grounds bravely. Brethren, believe me, these Christian natives of Abeokuta do not wish to keep the gospel to themselves. Already they have promised that teachers should be sent to other towns; nor do they fail, wherever they go, to speak of what they know. I am going back to my own land with great hope in my heart, feeling much blessed and encouraged and have only to ask that my many kind friends in England will continue to pray for me and for the salvation of my people.'** The applause from the meeting was rousing and they all gathered around to wish him and his wife Godsspeed back to West Africa.

Adjai and his family returned first to Freetown, where they were welcomed by the people who were pleased to see the return of one of their own from abroad. He was showered with invitations to preach at various churches. Here in this city where he was brought as a rescued slave boy and it is here in this city that he took his first steps towards learning the path towards Christianity. It was here also that he learned the alphabet, went to school and the Christian Institution of Fourah Bay, and it was also in this very place that he first set eyes on a young girl called Asano, who was later to become his wife and helpmate. Whilst in Freetown he was able to preach about his work in Abeokuta and to rouse interest in the people of Freetown.

They left Freetown and landed in Lagos for the first time, a place that was to evoke many memories of the last time he was at that place as a slave boy. He remembered how he had been terrified when he saw the sea for the first time and writes in his journal, **'I could recollect many places I knew during my captivity, so I went over the spots where slave barracoons used to be. What a difference; some of the spots are now converted into plantations with sheds full of maize and cassava, whilst others are filled with casks of palm oil and other merchandise, instead of slaves in chains and iron, in agony and despair.'**

After their stay in Lagos, the family had the long and difficult journey before them to reach Abeokuta. It was June 1852, and the rainy season had begun when they started for Abeokuta. Luckily, they reached their destination without any mishap. Adjai spent some time relating to the other missionaries his discussions in London, and his experience of meeting Queen Victoria and Prince Albert. He also continued working on the translation of the Old Testament into Yoruba. He was also to write grammars and vocabularies of the Ibo, Hausa and Nupe languages later on. The church he had built in Abeokuta was made of solid stone, large and boasting eight windows and on a given Sunday, was filled by a large congregation of over three hundred converts. The Sunday school also attracted a large number of children who came willingly to hear about Jesus. Before he left for England the church had needed some work to be done and as soon as he returned he organised the repair work.

AN INTERNAL ALBUM

OF NOTABLE

PHOTOGRAPHS

CHURCH MISSIONARY SOCIETY

BISHOPS ATTENDING THE LAMBETH
CONFERENCE OF BISHOPS IN 1888.
BISHOP SAMUEL ADJAI CROWTHER IS SITTED
THIRD FROM RIGHT

THE REV. HENRY VENN, THE FIRST AND
LONGEST SERVING SECRETARY OF THE CMS

THE REV. FREDERICK SCHON, FRIEND AND
MENTOR OF ADJAI

THE REV. SAMUEL CROWTHER AFTER
WHOM BISHOP SAMUEL ADJAI CROWTHER WAS NAMED

PALM COTTAGE, CANTERBURY
RD.GILLINGHAM, KENT - HOME OF THE REV
FREDERICH SCHON, MENTOR OF ADJAI WHERE THEY
CONSULTED ON ADJAI'S SELECTION AND HOME OF
SALLY FORBES BONETTA FROM 1855 TO 1861

FAMILY AND FRIENDS

DANDESON COATES CROWTHER -
SON OF ADJAI

THE BISHOP AND HIS SON

BISHOP SAMUEL ADJAI CROWTHER AND HIS CLERGYMEN

BISHOP SAMUEL ADJAI CROWTHER WITH SOME
OF HIS CLERGYMEN ON 12 JUNE 1873

THIS IMAGE INCLUDES HENRY JOHNSON, ARCHDEACON OF
THE UPPER NIGER (1878) AND JAMES JOHNSON, C.M.S.
MISSIONARY - WEST AFRICA

They were picnicking at the **'Wilberforce oak'**, at Keston in Kent, now part of Bromley borough. William Wilberforce (1759-1833), the politician and philanthropist, often visited the Prime Minister, William Pitt the younger (1759o-1806), who owned the Hollywood estate at Keston. Wilberforce's resolution, **'after a conversation in the open air at the root of an old tree at Holwood just above the steep descent into the vale of Keston,'** to give notice in the House of Commons of his intention to bring forward the abolition of the slave trade, is well known

MISSION AND DEATH

FOURAH BAY COLLEGE BUILDING, DESIGNED
BY A BRITISH ARCHITECT WITH FIREPLACES
AND CHIMNEYS

KING OCKIYA SURRENDERING ANCESTOR IDOLS
TO BISHOP ADJAI CROWTHER

DESCENDANTS OF BISHOP ADJAI
CROWTHER AT THE GRAVE OF ARCHDEACON
DANDESON COATES CROWTHER AND HIS WIFE
SARAH AT KISSY ROAD CEMETERY, FREETOWN

CHAPTER 7
ANOTHER EXPEDITION

A Mr. Macgregor Laird, a London merchant, had a long and extensive engagement with trade and commerce between England and West Africa. In the summer of 1853 he entered into a contract with the British Government to fit out and send a small steamer up the River Nun and Niger, in order to ascend the stream up to the confluence with the Tshadda and then to explore that branch of the river. The objectives of the expedition were to establish commercial relations with the native tribes and to find the explorers Heinrich Barth and Vogel, who had disappeared on an earlier expedition, trying to penetrate Africa from the north. **(The expedition did not however find Barth or Vogel, who had both crossed the upper reaches of the Niger. Vogel was murdered in 1855 and the report showed that he had crossed the River Benue).** It was decided that Her Majesty's Government would appoint certain officers to accompany the expedition, and Mr Laird was to provide for trade and batter with the natives. The risks and expenses were to be undertaken by Mr. Laird. He made the Committee of the Church Missionary Society (CMS) what was a most generous offer, of a free passage for a missionary to accompany the expedition. The committee asked Adjai whether he was willing to go on the expedition, and he readily agreed. One should remember that Adjai had been on earlier expedition up the River Niger in 1841, which had ended in near disaster. This expedition, he was assured, would be different.

The exploration of the River Niger and other rivers in Africa, had been undertaken by several Europeans before, with some perishing in the attempt. In 1805, the explorer Mungo Park perished trying to descend the Niger with three companions, the last survivors of the 38 men who had set out with him from the Gambia. In 1816 another expedition to navigate the Congo River by Captain Turkey, also failed and only one survivor returned to England.

Between 1821 and 1824 two European explorers Denham and Clapperton trying to reach the Soudan from the Mediterranean, also came to grief; they lost their leader, Dr. Oudney and other European members of the expedition. Undaunted by his earlier failure, again in 1825 Clapperton, with two companions Captain Pearce and Dr. Morrison, lost their lives trying to penetrate the continent from the Bight of Benin. Only his servant Richard Lander survived this expedition. That same year a Major Laing perished after reaching Timbuctoo. Not put off by these failures, in 1830 Richard Lander, the surviving servant of Clapperton and his brother John, managed to reach the Niger from Badagry, and by floating down discovered the embouchure on the Bight of Benin. Other expeditions, some successful and others abject failures, were made in 1832 and 1833 - the Liverpool Expedition and in 1836 and 1840. In 1845 the British Consul General, John Beecroft, based in Fernando Po, also made the ascent of the Niger, but with considerable loss of life.

But, this expedition, which Adjai was to join would be different and what's more, successful. This was to mark a new era in the exploration of Africa. As Macgregor Laird writing in a letter to the Earl of Clarendon, when trying to persuade the government to support the expedition said, *'for example with the advancement of medical research, some of the dreaded diseases that took its toll on the European explorers had been fairly met and conquered. Therefore, the plausible objection to exploring Africa, the risk of life, had been met.'*

As usual Adjai kept a meticulous journal of the expedition, which he published under the title *'Journal of an Expedition up the Niger and Tshadda'* in 1855 and in conjunction with J. C. Taylor, *'The Gospel on the Banks of the Niger 1857-1859.'* It is from these journals that we can find out what happened on the expedition.

On 13 June,1854, Adjai travelled from Abeokuta to Fernando Po, via Lagos to join the expedition on board the Pleiad to begin the journey up the Niger. He was accompanied by his son Samuel and a Mr Phillips, who were going to Lagos. He records that he took with him about seven hundred-weight of cotton, to be shipped from Lagos to Manchester. Also to join the expedition was Simon Jones, a Sierra Leonean, whose parents were Ibos and who was to act as interpreter during the journey.

The expedition was to have been led by John Beecroft, who, since 1849 had been the British Consul General for the Bights of Benin and Biafra, based in Fernando Po. During that period he had worked diligently to abolish the slave trade, and had looked after the welfare of the liberated slaves. He had also spent time exploring parts of the area along the Cross and Niger rivers and so had extensive knowledge of the area. He was also a friend of Adjai whom he had first met when he visited him in Abeokuta. Adjai records that as he knew no other person going on the expedition, this caused him a little anxiety, *'but I resigned everything to God's good and unerring providence.'*

On 20 June,1854, Adjai embarked on the Forerunner in Lagos, where he met the naturalist and Surgeon, Dr.William Baikie, who was also on the expedition. But, just before they sailed for Fernando Po, from where the expedition was to begin, tragedy struck. John Beecroft, who was well over sixty years of age, became ill suddenly, and not all the skills and medicine of the doctor could save him, and he died. He died just before Adjai reached Fernando Po, and as soon as he came ashore, he visited Beecroft's grave, which was on the point on the cliff, under a large cotton-tree, where he had directed that he be buried. As Adjai wrote in his journal of Sunday June 25, *'Thus ended the life of this useful person, after twenty-five years stay in Africa, during which period he had won the affection of the many people who knew his worth in the countries he had visited. The chiefs of Abeokuta had sent salutations and messages to him by me, which he did not live to receive. As long as this generation lasts, the name of Mr. Beecroft will not be forgotten in this part of West Africa. The people were very glad to see me, and expressed their regret for the loss of Mr Beecroft; for, he had made full preparation for the Expedition; he had engaged many intelligent natives who had been used to go up the Niger with him, and who were ready to go anywhere with him, they being mutually attached to each other, for he treated them as a father. It will be a long time before his place can be taken by another who will have the same interest in the country and its people like he did.'*

Although it seemed at first that without the leadership of Beecroft the expedition would be abandoned, they had not counted on Dr. Baikie. He stepped into the vacant position left by the death of Mr. Beecroft, and informed the other members, *'The Pleiad will continue its journey up the Niger and I know I can rely on you'*. And rely on him they did, and he did not fail them as he proved himself a man of great leadership skills. The expedition embarked on the Pleiad on the afternoon of July 8, with two large iron canoes laden with coal in tow, and lasted from July to November, just four months in 1854. And it is from the journal of Adjai and his letters that we learn something about what took place on the expedition. For as soon as he returned from the expedition he wrote to his mentor, the Reverend Henry Venn, Secretary to the Committee of the Church Missionary Society in London. In a letter dated 2 December,1854, he gives some details of what went on:

'You will, no doubt be glad to hear that we have returned from the Niger in good health and spirits, a singular instance, without any death, among the Europeans, twelve in number, or among the fifty-four Africans, either from sickness or accident. The Expedition was in the

river exactly sixteen weeks, the very day it returned to the Nun. We commenced our ascent of the Tshadda on 7 August, and the last point we were able to reach was Gurowa, above Bomanda, a port of Hamaruwa, about 300 miles from the confluence of the Kowara and Tshadda, on 22 September, when we were completely out of fuel, no wood being obtainable within three or four miles of the river bank. This was the only difficulty we met with, and which prevented our reaching the confluence of the Binue and Faro, where it was crossed by Dr. Barth, and, according to all the accounts we have received, could not have been more than 100 miles from Hamaruwa. It could be reached in five days' journey on foot, travelling by the course of the river, but dangerous on account of unsubdued natives, and ten days' journey by a circuitous route around the Fumbina mountains, which was said to be safer. The reception we met with all along from Kings and chiefs of the countries on the Binua was beyond expectation. We made two visits to Mohamma, the Sultan of Hamaruwa, fourteen miles from the river, in both of which we were most respectfully received and entertained by the Sultan.

We returned to Aboh on 31 October, and met Simon Jones, whom we had left there, quite well and much respected by all, both chiefs and people. He moved about among them with perfect freedom and made several trips up river, to Ossamare, Onitsha and Asaba markets, and to an interior town called Oko-Ala, on the back of Aboh, of about a days' journey; the chef of which placed, asked Simon Jones, why we always stopped at Aboh, and never paid him a visit; to which Jones replied that there will not be a place left unvisited in the time. He was about three days absent from Aboh, when he returned for fear the steamer might have arrived.

Simon Jones spoke to them of the folly of their superstitious customs, and he said, the one of chewing sticks to clean their teeth in the morning and spouting the spittle before their country fashion invoking his blessing upon those who wish him good, and imprecating his anger upon those who desire their hurt, was giving up by some of them as his speaking to them of his folly of so doing. He was the companion of Tshukuma and Aje, although he paid them due respect. Having found this favourable state of things in Aboh, I took steps to secure a parcel of grounds for a contemplated Mission station, to prevent the spot being spoiled by the people, and gave Aje strict charge to keep the people away from it. My further proceedings in Aboh will be seen more fully in my journal to that place. I have furnished the Bishop of Sierra Leone with a copy of my journals to Aboh for fuller information; and I have suggested to Dr Baikie the advantage of taking Simon Jones to Sierra Leone, to give his Lordship verbal information of Aboh country from actual knowledge of three months stay among them. I have taken these steps from the instruction I had received from the Bishop, to ascertain what reception Native Teachers would meet with in Aboh'.

Adjai was very keen for the word of God to be extended to as many of the native tribes as possible, as he stated in the letter to the Rev. Henry Venn:

'I believe the time is fully come when Christianity must be introduced on the banks of the Niger: the people are willing to receive any who may be sent among them. The English are still looked upon as friends, with whom they themselves desire to have connection as with the first nation of the world. Could the work have been begun since 1841, how imperfect it may have been, yet it would have kept up the thread of connection with England and the countries on the banks of the Niger. God has provided instruments to begin the work, in the Liberated Africans in the Colony of Sierra Leone, who are the natives of the banks of this river.

If this time is allowed to pass away, the generation of the liberated teachers who are immediately connected with the present generation of the natives of the interior will pass away with it also. Many intelligent men who took deep interest in the introduction of trade and Christianity by the Niger, who have been known to the people, have died since; so have many of the chiefs and the people in the country who were no less interested to be brought in connection with England by seeing their liberated countrymen return. Had not Simon Jones been with us, who is well-known to Obi and his sons, we should have had some difficulty in gaining the confidence of the people of Aboh at our ascent.'

Writing in his journal, Adjai recorded everything about the expedition, which started on 13 June,1854, the day he left Abeokuta for Lagos to join the Expedition to Explore the Tshadda, from Fernando Po and ended on November 7, five months later when the expedition returned to Fernando Po from where it had started. When the expedition returned they held a service of Thanksgiving for its successful completion without any loss of life, and for surviving the many hardships and without any person being worse from either sickness or accident. Adjai ended his journal with these words on November 7:

'Fernando Po was in sight this morning; about five pm, we dropped anchor in Clarence Grove. We soon landed, and were received by Rev. Diboll, the Baptist Missionary, and all the native settlers, having been boarded by Mr. Mackenzie a short time before. When we landed, we were received by Governor Lysander with heartfelt gratitude that we all have been spared to return from the river in good health and spirits. May this singular instance of God's favour and protection drive us nearer to the Throne of Grace, to humble ourselves before our God, whose instrument we are, and who can continue to dispense with our services, as it seems good to His unerring wisdom.'

In the journal, we read about some of the mishaps and vicissitudes that befell the expedition. Soon after leaving Fernando Po, the spindle of the safety valve of the Pleiad broke and the ship drifted towards the mouth of the Bonny river, but after it was fixed they had to cross the flood tide of the river. At one stage they took a wrong turning in the river, but they safely crossed over, piloted by Thomas Richards, a Yoruba man who had made many voyages up the Niger with Mr Beecroft and had good knowledge of the peculiarities of the coast of the Niger. But, they did not cross without mishap as one of the hawsers of one of the canoes, which carried the coal and wood for the ship, broke down. The ship could not offer any assistance, but they did cross the bar safely eventually.

During the expedition, they had to contend with some hostile tribes, malaria, lack of coal and wood to fire the engines, the ship stranded on sandbanks, lack of navigable water on the river, or fast flowing rivers, the effects of the slave raiders on the population and wily and cheating chiefs, who tried to extract as much as they could from the expedition in order to give them easy access on the river. But, during all these vicissitudes and setbacks, Adjai and the others never deviated from their mission, to bring the word of God to the locals and to bring commerce and trade to them. Every Sunday, church services were held wherever they happened to be, either on the ship, or on shore. They had brought clothes, cowries and other goods which they exchanged for food such as sheep, butter and root vegetables. Clothes were particularly in great demand and could be exchanged for high value goods. They did come across several tribes, such as the Fulani, Hausa and Yoruba, some friendly and welcoming and some not. But, they persevered and returned safely, and as Adjai put it 'without any death, or sickness, or accident.'

On 21July, 1854, they stopped of at Aboh. There they learned that the old King Obi had died. During the early expedition in 1851, Adjai had met king Obi and promised him that they would return. But, they never did even though the king had promised friendship to the white man. He had hoped they would return before he died, lamenting the fact that 'the white man has forgotten me and his promise'. The new ruler was the one of his three sons who were in dispute which of them was to take over the kingship. They hoped that the arrival of the white men would solve the dispute and tell them which one should reign. But, the expedition refused to get involved. For It seems as if the rightful heir was the eldest son Tshukuma and it was to him that the party went to negotiate. From the pen of Adjai we learn about the substance of the negotiation with the new king:

'The substance of Mr. Baikie's interview with the chief was that the Queen had desired him to visit them and see how they did, and we were sorry to hear of Obi's death - we hoped his successor would be of the same as the late king- and they still adhered to the treaty he had signed with Captain Trotter, who had acted in the name of the Queen: and that trade was now come to Aboh country. Tshukuma replied that he was very pleased to see the large ship come again to Abo and that he and the other headmen were particularly charged by Obi before his death not to deviate from the path he had trod respecting his friendship with the white men, and that they would act accordingly. But, as his brother Aje was absent with a large number of headmen, so in

order to settle the matter, he expressed the wish that we wait until he returned.'

When Adjai spoke, he told the king that they were keen to establish a mission in Aboh as they had done at Badagry, Abeokuta, Calabar and Bonney and was pleased when one of daughters of the king, said that she could not see why they should establish missions in these places and not in Aboh. He informed them that the CMS had long been thinking of sending teachers to Aboh, to reside there and teach them many things if they are willing to learn. He told them about the sacrifices that the Lord Jesus had made for the sins of the world and that these sacrifices shone some light on darkness, ignorance and superstitions. During this lecture Adjai kept on repeating the names 'Oparra Tshuku! Oparra Tshuku, which means Son of God! Son of God. Before the expedition departed from Aboh, they left Simon Jones to help establish the mission.

At the end of the expedition, Adjai returned to Abeokuta, via Ibadan where he held a conference with Mr & Mrs Hinderer and with Mr Mann at Ijeye, about the expansion of the mission in Yoruba country and elsewhere. Mr Gollmer, who had been with him in establishing the Christian mission in Abeokuta and was then in Lagos, was recalled to London, and Adjai was sent to take his place in Lagos. It was here that he continued to work on his translations of the Bible into Yoruba, and also prepared a primer, a vocabulary and extracts from the Bible into the Ibo language. In a letter to the CMS in London, from Abeokuta dated January 1855 about the expedition he had just returned from, he ends with these words, '*I cannot bring these notices to a close without again pressing the necessity of immediate steps being taken, when another Expedition ascends the river, to locate some persons of the Ibo nation in the town of Abo, and, if possible, also some Christian teachers at the Confluence of the Kowara and Tshadda; the latter is a nucleus of trade between the natives of the interior, and the situation is most important. When two or three yearly visits in succession are made by steam-ships, there will be mutual understanding between Britain and the inhabitants of the Delta, the river will be opened for our boats and canoes, as the Ogun is at present with us in Abeokuta. It is my belief and I do not express it from a momentary excitement, that the Niger Mission may yearly be visited by prudent and experienced Missionaries from the Yoruba country. It only requires that seasonable opportunity be seized to open the way, and keep a chain of communication between this and the Niger, so that in case there is no opportunity of visiting it by steam from the sea, the Mission will not be neglected, when it can be visited by the land route.*'

At the end of the expedition, in a letter to Adjai from Fernando Po dated 28 November, 1854 Dr. Baikie writes:

'After having been together for upwards of four months, closely engaged in exploring Central Africa, I cannot allow you to depart without expressing to you, in the warmest manner, the pleasure I derived from your

company, and acknowledging the information I have reaped from you.

Your long and intimate acquaintance with native tribes, with your general knowledge of their customs, particularly fit you for a journey such as we have now returned from, and I cannot but feel that your advice was always readily granted to me, nor had I ever the smallest reason to repent having followed it. It is nothing more than a simple fact that no slight portion of the success we met with in our intercourse with the tribes is due to you.

Our voyage has providentially terminated, so far favourably, and without loss of life. You are now about to return to the scene of your past labours and to resume your share of the work for civilising and regenerating a vast territory. That your labours may continue to meet with success and that you may be spared to see your exertions bearing good fruit, is the earnest and sincere wish of, yours faithfully, W. B. Baikie.'

CHAPTER 8
ANOTHER EXPEDITION

As Adjai points out in the previous letter, the time was ripe for another expedition to be mounted in order to establish more Christian missions along the Niger river. The CMS in London listened to him, and appealed to Lord Palmerstone for help from the Government to mount such an expedition to the Niger. It was first envisaged that different Christian missions were to be established along the Niger, and so in 1857 the ship Dayspring left England bound for West Africa. The ship was to first call in Freetown, where Adjai had by then returned, to collect him, Bishop Weeks, his old guardian, the Rev. Mr. Frey, a hard working mission staff, Mr. Beale who had been working with Adjai on the expedition, and Dr. Baikie. They were to be accompanied by half a dozen local ministers. But, even before the ship arrived, Bishop Weeks, after labouring in the work of the Lord on the coast for many years, and who with his wife had been the first guardians of Adjai, died. Adjai was devastated as he owed him much for his life. For it was he, with his wife, who had shown him much kindness when as a recaptured slave boy, he first arrived in Freetown, for his mentoring and was responsible for his training and life, which had brought him to where he was now. His death was followed by that of Mr. Frey and later on by Mr. Beale's. As Adjai wrote in his diary, *'The late floods of affliction upon the West African mission are overwhelming. The removal of good Bishop Weeks, and that of Mr. Beale and Mr. Frey, so soon after both had just returned from their visit to the Bight of Benin and the Gold Coast, calls for prayers and to the humiliation before our God, who is the dispenser of these painful dispensa - tions. Perhaps we have been sacrificing to the nets and the drag instead of to Him, who has said, "Cast the net on the right of the ship." May our sins be forgiven and our errors corrected in the judgement and not in anger.'*

Thus the expedition was not able to spare any of the local ministers, and the ship sailed with Adjai, Dr. Baikie, Rev. J. C. Taylor, Simon Jones, an old friend of his from the earlier expedition, and two young men who had been residing in the house of Mr. Schon. So, it was a much depleted group that sailed on the 'Dayspring' that day. Rev. Taylor was a Sierra Leonean whose parents had been born in Ibo land, and who himself spoke Ibo. He had been a student at the Fourah Bay Institute, and had been ordained a priest. Adjai also took with him Kasumo, a Yoruba Mohammedan and a liberated African, who had been an Arabic teacher for many years. The reason for this addition to the party he explained thus, *'I had it advisable, with a view of making favourable impressions on the minds of the Mohammedan population through which we pass to Sokoto and Ilorin, to engage Kasumo, to accompany me on my travels. He has however appreciated the benevolence of the British government on behalf of Africa, nor less so the labours of the Church Missionary Society in converting the heathen from idolatry to the worship of the true God. Such a man would do a vast deal in softening the bigotry and prejudice of men of his persuasion. The beginning of our missionary operations under Mohammedan government should not be disputes about the truth or falsehood of one religion, or other, but we should at toleration, to be permitted to teach their heathen subjects the religion we profess.'*

We find from the journal kept by Adjai, this was to be the first and most important of the Niger Christian missions established by the CMS in the territory. The importance of the expedition should not be under estimated, even though it came to an abrupt halt in a place called Rabbah further up the Niger, yet it was from the *'Dayspring'* that the first stations were planted by the Niger mission.

According to Adjai, the aim was to establish the first mission at a place called Abo. The old King Obi had showed that he was willing to accept the Europeans as guests. The king, whom Adjai had met on an earlier expedition in 1845 was now dead and there was infighting for the kingship between his two sons Tshukuma and Aje. Tshukuma being the older son, had more claim to the throne, but he lacked the energy of his brother Aje. Tshukuma was favourably disposed towards the mission, but the other brother Aje, was another matter. He was impertinent towards the missionaries, had bad manners, was greedy and demanded gifts such as Adjai's slippers and the ship's dinner bell. Adjai, with much sweet talking, was able to secure a piece of land for the mission, but not before pacifying Aje with a pink cock hat and a gaudy umbrella. Adjai made this note in his journal about him, *'Aje with all his wives dressed in ships' bunting, tried to make an impression of his greatness, and what was much more serious, opposed and interfered in every way, the establishment of the mission in his country. Before quitting Abo for the present I think it is right and just to say a word in in favour of Aje's faithfulness in one respect, whatever his failings may be in other matters. It will be remembered through an imposition in 1854, during the expedition up the Niger and Tshadda organised by Macgregor Laird, that the prisoners who were confined and would have been either killed or sold for their offences, were then released. Since that time they had never been touched, and really pardoned, according to Aje's promise to us. One of these men on seeing me, fell on his knees in thankfulness for his deliverance, and on the return of his companion, who had been absent, they brought me some palm wine as an acknowledgment of their gratitude. Had not these men introduced themselves three years after it might have been doubted whether Aje had fulfilled his promise.'*

The next stop for the '*Dayspring*' was the town of Onitsha, about one hundred and forty miles up the Niger from Abo. At first the people were not too friendly, but they soon relaxed when it appeared that the visitors came in peace. The king received them cordially and listened attentively to their proposal and plans to set up a mission in his territory. The King then informed his people what the visitors wanted to do and asked whether they approved, or not. The people agreed and a spot was found on which to construct the Mission building. Also, a house was rented to prepare for a factory.

Adjai noted that houses in the town were arranged in groups of twenty-six, with each group consisting of 250 persons. He, therefore, estimated that the whole town to have a population of just short of 6500 people.

But, human sacrifice and cannibalism was still on going in the king's domain, as Adjai noted in his journal, *'one day as we entered the Kings' palace, there was great rejoicing, beating of drums, dancing and frantic gestures and moving. When we came to our lodging, one of the headmen paid us a visit, and I asked him the cause of this amusement, and was told it was in honour of the burial of a relative of the landlord who died six months ago. Simon Jones, who remained ashore last night, had heard that a human sacrifice was to be made to the names of the dead, and he told the people of the wickedness of the practice. On my putting the question as to the cause of the amusement, the headman was conscience stricken, and told Simon Jones that the victim had not yet been killed. We then took the opportunity, and spoke most seriously to the headman in the hearing of many people who stood in the square, of the abomination of this wicked practice, the more so, as the victim was a poor, blameless, female slave. He then assured us that he had not known that it was wrong to do so; but, as we had now told them, the human sacrifice should not be performed, but a bullock should be killed in its stead. He proposed that we should buy the woman, that they might buy the bullock with the cowries in her stead. This we refused to do, as we were not slave traders. He then said that the woman should be sold to somebody else, which we thought was better than to kill her. Before we returned to the ship, Simon Jones was told that the poor woman was loosed from her bonds.'*

When the ship sailed for its next port of call, Mr. Taylor and Simon Jones remained behind to prepare the work for the establishment of the mission at Onitsha. This included showing the people the correct ways for cultivating and growing of cassava, Indian corn and fruit trees around the mission building.

The *Dayspring* sailed up the Niger calling at various places, some friendly and some not. When they reached Idda, a town standing on a high cliff, and overlooking the confluence of the Kworra and Tshadda rivers, they were admitted, with much heathen dignity into the presence of the Atta dressed in rich-silk-velvet robes sitting on a throne. After much discussion, in the presence of the dowager queen, who sympathised with their cause, a favourable site was selected for a mission building. They also reached Galadima, a mostly Muslim place, Gbede, Lokoja and Eggan, all Nupe country, where the old chief remembered the 1841 expedition. They were able to establish missions in these places. At a place called Fo-Fo, the mate of the *Dayspring* breathed his last and was buried on the beach.

Sailing up the river to Rabbah, with its dangerous and rock strewn rapids the *'Dayspring,'* which had carried them from Fernando Po through many a dangerous parts of the Niger, also breathed its last, as it struck a rock at Jebba and quickly sank.

Adjai and all abroad her, were only able to grab a few things before safely managing to reach the shore. They put up makeshift tents and mats, and under much discomfort they managed to survived for several months. During their enforced stay, Adjai did not sit idly by, but made use of the time by trying to study the Nupe Language. In his journal he wrote, *'I engaged Ibrahima, a native of Jebby, a Mohammedan, who is a master of both Nupe and Hausa languages, as my teacher. My servant, Henry who speaks Nupe and Hausa a little, becomes most useful, as he also speaks English and Yoruba. Ibrahim speaks a little Yoruba also. Thus we have the advantage of three languages, viz, the English, the Hausa and the Yoruba, to fix the fourth, which is Nupe: and as this is carefully done, much error cannot creep into the work.'*

Their sprits where high as they knew they would be rescued by another ship, the *Sunbeam* which they knew was following. They made themselves as comfortable as they could, and short of food, they lived on wild honey and corn. Dr Baikie was able to advise them on how to take care of themselves. Added to their discomfiture, the tribes whose hands they had unwittingly fallen, were not too friendly and wild breast roamed nearby on the lookout for food. But with the help of God, whose work they had come to do, they survived until October when the *Sunbeam* came to their rescue.

WRECK OF THE SUNBEAM

On their way back down river, Adjai stopped off at Onitsha to see how the work of the new mission was progressing. He was sad to say farewell to Dr. Baikie and his travelling companions with whom he had shared so many adventures. Dr. Baikie thanked him for his excellent help on the expedition and said they would meet again either in Lagos or Abeokuta.

Adjai was very pleased with the work that Mr Taylor and Simon Jones had done in Onitsha during his absence. They had built the mission house and church, and constructed a school, which was very well attended. Mr. Taylor also kept a comprehensive journal of his time in Onitsha from which we see how much work he and Simon Jones put into establishing the mission there. The work was not all plain-sailing however, as he found the chiefs unwilling to help, but luckily found the people more open to hear the gospel and the word of God. He had many runs striving against entrenched superstitious practices amongst the people of Onitsha, but overcame them. He gave several examples of this, including his fight against the practice of killing all children who happen to be born twins. The mother is also degraded and treated cruelly. He records one such case when a woman who had converted to Christianity gave birth to twin girls. Her friends, not wanting to sacrifice the two little girls, sent for Mr Perry the minister. He said at once 'Destroy them not, for a blessing is on them.' And despite the anger of a furious mob of five hundred men armed to the teeth with guns, cutlasses, spears, clubs, bows and arrows who surrounded the mission compound, demanding that the babies be given up to them.' The little ones were safely conveyed to the safety of the English ship *Wanderer* on the Niger and saved from destruction.

Much to the sorrow of Adjai and Mr. Taylor and all who laboured at the mission in Onitsha, his loyal and long standing friend Simon Jones died in Fernando Po. They had first met in 1841 during his first expedition, and again in 1854 during his second expedition up the Niger. Simon Jones was a Sierra Leonean who had acted as interpreter on both expeditions, and had remained friends and spiritual colleagues with Adjai since then. His loss was not only the great loss of a Christian colleague, but also because of his translating skills in several languages of the local tribes. Taylor records the following on the Sunday of his death: *'This morning a woman came into my residence and requested me to follow her, for she wanted to see me particularly. I got myself ready and went with her. After walking about two miles we came to a very beautiful sand beach, where to my surprise I found twenty-four women and four men. One of them rose up and said, 'Sir, we expressly sent for you to preach to us the Word of God: do, for we thirst to hear God's living word: please sir, help us.' I stood under a hollow tree, and told them I was sorry I had no book with me. To my great surprise each one brought out a hymn book. I then gave out that beautiful hymn, 'Jesus, where'er Thy people meet'; and I took one of their Bibles, and expounded the words of the Apostle Paul from Acts xvi. 13: And on the Sabbath we went out of the city by a riverside, where prayer was wont to be made; and we sat down, and spoke unto the women which resorted thither. Thank God for this opportunity.'*

After seeing the splendid work that Taylor and Simon Jones had done in Onitsha, in 1858 Adjai then took a rather perilous journey back to Abeokuta and Lagos in a roundabout way. First, he took a canoe to make a three hundred miles journey to Rabbah, where the *Dayspring* had sank. He was able to set up a mission there. From there it was overland to Ilorin, the capital of the Hausas' north of the country and from there to Abeokuta. It is not sure many men at that time, had made such a journey, first by canoe and then by foot, and recorded it. He must be the first. It was not an auspicious time for travellers through the bush, as some of the tribes were hostile to each other and were at constant war.

For example Abeokuta and Ilorin were allies with other towns, against Ibadan and Oyo. But, for a man of God this was no problem for Adjai, and he safely made it to Abeokuta where he was reunited with Dr Baikie. He did not stay long but soon was on his way again, this time to Lagos to be reunited with his wife and family early in 1859.

Adjai was able to open missions in Akassa and Bonny in 1861 and was invited to open one at Idda in 1867. He stationed two Sierra Leonean catechists in Bonny, and asked them to begin the study of the language. In the 1870s we find Adjai still travelling up and down the Niger establishing new missions and visiting ones already up and ready. Apart from Onitsha, Bonny and Akassa he founded the missions in Igbere, Lokoja, Abonema and Bunguma. When the British Consulate was closed in Fernando Po in 1869, no further gun boats entered the Niger for some time, and in order to get around the new missions, Adjai had to rely on passing trading vessels. It was not until 1878 that the CMS. was able to provide him with a ship of his own, just like providing a company car today, to enable him to continue with his mission work. The paddle steamer was named appropriately - *The Henry Venn*, after the Secretary of the of the CMS in London, one of the early champions of Adjai and his mission work.

MISSION STEAMER - HENRY VENN

It was built in the shipbuilding yards on the River Clyde in Scotland, and paid for by subscription by the Christian people in Britain, who admired the missionary work he was doing. This provided much needed transport for visiting the various mission stations along the Niger.

The CMS also provided the ageing Adjai with two Archdeacons to help him with his duties. One was his son Dandeson, who had followed his illustrious father into the church. He had been sent to England to study at the CMS College in Islington, and on 19 June, 1870 had received his ordination at the hands of his father at St Mary's Parish Church, Islington. The ordination was unique in that it was the first time that a black bishop had ordained his black son. According to the records of the church a large congregation had gathered for this unique occasion and was followed with deepest attention. The Bishop chose as his text for his sermon, *2 Timothy 11, verse 23*, and drew attention to the parallel between temporal and spiritual conflict, and solemnly committed to his son the responsibility and yet privilege of waging a brave warfare against sin under the banner of the cross.

Dandeson was put in charge of the mission at Bonny for the Delta area, and the other, a Sierra Leonean Henry Johnson, was put in charge of the upper stations. When Henry Johnson reached his station on the Niger, he started to study the Nupe language, and became quite a linguist and an authority in the language. In 1882 he published a reading book in the language, in 1883 a catechism, in 1886 and in 1887 a translations of all the four Gospels. Most of these were printed on a printing press which was installed at Bonny. Dandeson also made some contribution to publishing for in 1881, he compiled an account of the languages of the lower Niger, mainly from already published materials.

CHAPTER 9
A BISHOP AT LAST

The West Coast of Africa was once plagued by disease, especially malaria, for Europeans. It is said that the average lifespan for a white person in Sierra Leone, in particular, was two years. Many died, even before then. Within several years, the Anglican church in Sierra Leone lost three Bishops due to the disease. The first was Bishop Vidal, who was succeeded by Bishop Weeks, who although he had a long useful knowledge of the colony, succumbed to the dreaded fever after only two years. His replacement was Dr Bowen, who was transferred from the Holy Land to take his place. He was in the post for also only two years when he went to meet his maker. So, in very quick succession Sierra Leone had and lost three bishops. This must have brought on a headache for the CMS in London, and it is thought that it was Henry Venn, the Secretary of the society who had the brilliant idea that, perhaps, it would be a good policy if the post was to be filled by a local native clergyman. He was a brilliant man of great vision, foresight and a forward-looking man for his time. He had always believed that the African could spread the Gospel in his own country much better, rather than Europeans whose life spans were limited by the attack of disease and fever.

An article which appeared in the Church Missionary Intelligentsia in May 1864, stated that it was about time that a native Bishopric was created in West Africa. The article went on to say:

"The opportune moment thus appears to have arrived when the native church should be further empowered to go forthwith and with a holy freedom to do the Lord's work in Africa and the native ministry be permitted to culminate in a native episcopate. The question is, can one among the African clergymen be found to whom so great a responsibility can with safety be trusted? And this question the Church Missionary Society has ventured to answer in the affirmative. Nearly twenty-one years have elapsed since the Reverend Samuel Crowther was ordained a deacon by the late Bishop of London. The Lord had given him grace during the period, which has since elapsed to continue humble, consistence and useful. He has made full proof of his ministry. The new missions on the Niger imperatively require episcopal superintendents. They are so remote from the Bishop of Sierra Leone as to be placed entirely beyond his reach. The native catechists who have been instrumental in raising up the Onitsha and Grebe missions require prompt admission to Holy Oders, that they may duly minister to their flock and as well by the teaching of God's word as by the due administration of the Sacraments, promote their growth. Our Christians on the banks of the Niger need to be as quickly as possible brought forward into activity and be utilised in missionary effort among their countrymen. To delay any longer the native episcopate would be unduly to retard the development of the native church.'

As early as 1842, a report by the committee of the Fourah Bay Institute Building Fund, stressed the importance of the training of native priest to take over the work of the European missionaries, whose lifespan working in Africa were short. In its report it states, *'The important and cheering fact has been established, that both Chiefs and the people are willing to receive instructions from Black men, even from such as they know to have been in a state of slavery; that such Black men, trained in the Schools and Institution of the Society in Sierra Leone are capable of imparting it.'*

The Rev. Schon referred to this same subject in a letter after the failure of the expedition, in which he states, *'I have frequently had occasion to allude, in my journal, to the utility of the Native Agency. It demonstrates to us that the design for which the Expedition has been chiefly undertaken will, in the course of events, be carried out by Natives.'*

So, early in 1864 Adjai and his wife were surprised to receive a letter from Henry Venn requesting him to travel to London to attend a special meeting of the Committee of the Church Missionary Society. Adjai had no idea that the God he had worshiped and served since he became a Christian, had a plan for him to serve the church in a higher capacity. At the meeting in London, he was questioned repeatedly about the work of his mission and the plans he had for extending his work to areas in West Africa rather than only in Sierra Leone. He told the assembled great and good of the society, about the need for more missionaries and for the training of more local men to eventually be ordained as priest. He did not know that he was being interviewed for a position in the church, which some at the meeting was doubtful he was up to fulfilling.

So, he was shocked when Venn mentioned to all assembled at the meeting, that he knew just the right person who could take the lead in putting into practice some of the ideas he had mentioned. And that person, he said, should be Adjai. And whats more, he added, he was going to propose that Adjai be made bishop to take on the role of leading the flock in West Africa. Adjai was shocked and flabbergasted, and tried to talk himself out of the position, saying he did not think he was worthy of such a high office, and needed time to think about it. He would have liked to discuss the matter with his wife, but she was not with him and there was no way of communicating with her so far away in Sierra Leone. Luckily for him, his old friend Rev James Schon was in England and he went to consult him. Schon was living in Palm Cottage in Canterbury Street, in Gillingham, Kent. He stayed there for two days, during which time Schon was able to remove any doubts Adjai had, and assured him that he would make a fine bishop. So Adjai, after praying and fasting for several days, went and informed Venn of his acceptance of the position. Many years later, he related to his son Dandeson, what took place when he returned to Salisbury Square to inform Venn if his decision. As his son said later, he never related this to him without the deepest emotion.

On entering Mr Venn's room, he rose, made me sit down, put his hands on my shoulders and said, 'I hope you have brought me good news today.' Seeing no signs of good tidings, he took hold of both my hands, and looking me straight into my eyes, he said solemnly: 'Samuel Adjai, my son, will you deny me my last wish asked of you before I die?' This broke me down altogether, and with tears in my eyes I answered, 'It is the Lord, let Him do what seemeth Him good.' We both then knelt down and prayed together, with Mr Venn sobbing in gratitude.

And so, on 24 June, 1864, St Peter's Day one hundred and fifty years ago, at Canterbury Cathedral, Samuel Adjai Crowther, at the age of fifty-four was consecrated Bishop of the West African countries beyond British Jurisdiction.

It must have been an exceptional and joyous ceremony, the only fly in the ointment being that his wife and children were not there to witness this unique ceremony. But, he was overjoyed to see Mrs Weeks, his old teacher who had taught him to read and write, present at the ceremony. Sadly, her husband, who had returned to Freetown as Bishop of Sierra Leone in 1856, had died there, and was not alive to witness the consecration. It is said that just before the consecration started an elderly lady was seen making her way to a front seat. But, one of the wardens told her that these seats were reserved for distinguished guests who had tickets. She turned round and said in a clear voice, *'I think I have a right equally to this seat, because that black Minister to be consecrated Bishop this morning, was taught the alphabet by me,'* What joy it must have been for her to see the result of the compassion and love she and her husband had shown to a little slave boy all those years before. Also amongst the congregation was the then Captain, now Admiral, Harry Leeke, who was the captain of the *Myrmidon* the ship that had intercepted the Portuguese slave ship in whose hold was the young slave boy.

MYRMIDON

Adjai had met him on an earlier visit. Whilst working on the translation of the bible at the Church Missionary House library, he had recognised the man standing near him, and introduced himself as the slave boy he had rescued all those years previously. The then Sir Henry Leeke remembered him well, and invited him to his country house for the weekend. While there he preached in the local church.

Special trains were run from London and elsewhere, to bring people to witness the ceremony of the consecration of the first black bishop in the Anglican Communion. The ceremony must have been a sight to behold, as the Archbishop of Canterbury, assisted by five other bishops, entered the cathedral to the singing of the choir swelled by the voices of the congregation. As Archbishop Charles Thomas Langley intoned the words of the License, which had been promulgated by Her Majesty, *'We do by this our license under our Royal signet and sign manual authorise and empower you the said Samuel Adjai Crowther to be Bishop of the United Church of England and Ireland in the said countries of Western Africa beyond the limits of our dominion'* But, despite this limitation, his dominion was vast, and included countries in the whole of West Africa, but excluding the small British colonies such as Sierra Leone. For as it turned out to be, the white missionaries were not willing to serve under him, and so they continued to be responsible to the Bishop of Sierra Leone. How proud Adjai must have been to hear those sacred words, and how humble for a slave boy to reach this position in the Anglican church. He was not the only one to receive the solemn rites of congregation that day. There was also the new bishop of Tasmania and the new bishop of Peterborough.

The consecration was most favourably reported by the press of the day. The Church Times reported in its edition of 2 July, 1864 under the heading: CONSECRATION OF THREE BISHOPS IN CANTERBURY CATHEDRAL.

It was on St Peter's Day, in the year 1688 that the six bishops were acquitted after their memorable trial in Westminster Hall. The wonderful progress made since that period by the

Church, which was then in such danger, was strikingly evinced on this St Peter's Day, when in the venerable Cathedral here, three clergymen were consecrated bishops. One of these, the Rev. Francis Jeune, D.C.L. late Master of Pembroke College, Oxford and Dean of Lincoln, is appointed to an English diocese, that of Peterborough; another the Rev. Charles Henry Bromby, DD. late Principal of Cheltenham Training College, to a Colonial diocese, that of Tasmania, and the third, the Rev. Samuel Adjai Crowther, DD. to the missionary bishopric for the Niger district in Africa, of which country he is a native and where he has longed laboured as a missionary. The ancient city presented a very animated appearance, as not only did a large number of inhabitants and visitors from the immediate neighbourhood evince great anxiety to witness the proceedings, but a special train on the London, Chatham and Dover line brought many from the metropolis.

Morning Prayers were said at 8 o'clock, and at half- past eleven the most important proceedings of the day commenced, every part of the sacred edifice being completely filled. At that time the procession entered, comprising the choir, the dean, canons and clergy of the cathedral, with the Archbishop of Canterbury, the Bishops of Winchester, Lincoln, Gloucester and Bristol, Victoria (Hong Kong) and Bishop Nixon, late of Tasmania.

The Archbishop then commenced the Communion service, the Epistle being read by the

Bishop of Lincoln, the Gospel by the Bishop of Winchester; after the Nicene Creed, which was sung by the choir, the Rev. H. Longueville Mansel, Professor of Philosophy at Oxford, preached an eloquent sermon from the second and third verses of the third chapter of the second Epistle of St. Peter.

The choir then sang Mendelssohn's anthem, 'How lovely are the Messengers,' whilst the bishops elect retired to be vested in their rochets

.

BISHOP SAMUEL ADJAI CROWTHER WEARING
HIS ROCHETS

On their return they were met and presented as follows: Dr. Jeune, by the Bishops of Lincoln and Winchester: Dr Bromby, by Bishop Nixon and the Bishop of Victoria and Dr Crowther by the Bishops of Winchester and Gloucester and Bristol. The Letters Patent and License to consecrate were read by the registrar, the usual oaths administered, and the consecration service proceeded as far as the conclusion of the questions. The choir then sang Wise's anthem, 'Prepare Ye the way of the Lord', while the bishops designate retired to be fully robed.

Upon their return, whilst kneeling at the alter rails, the *'Veni Creator' was beautifully sung to Tallis's music and, after a prayer the most impressive and solemn part of the ceremony took place. The Archbishop and assistant bishops advanced to the alter rail and extended their right hands so that all rested in turn upon the head of each of the three new bishops, whilst in a clear and distinct voice, which reached into every part of the cathedral, his grace pronounced the solemn declaration and exhortation prescribed by the Prayer Book. Upon the conclusion of the consecration service the new bishops took their places within the rails, and the archbishop read the offertory sentences whilst the alms of the congregation were being collected.*

THE LAYING OF HANDS ON THE NEW BISHOPS
AT THE CONSECRATION CEREMONY

The 'Record', in a leading article was the first to point at the racism which was raising even at the time. *We might dwell on the practical refutation afforded by Dr. Crowther's merited elevation to the episcopate to the taunts of certain professors who maintain that the cerebral development of the Negro shows that he is disqualified for intellectual pursuits and that he cannot be lifted out of his congenital dullness; but, we pass on to entreat the prayers of wisdom, peculiar grace, and constant strength. Humanly speaking, the future of the native church depends on the manner in which its first Bishop shall administer its policy and organise its laws. It will be necessary for him to exercise great discrimination in conferring Holy Orders on his brethren and to take heed that he magnifies his office in the examination of all by the exemplary consistency of his life and the holiness of his conversation. That he will do so, we are assured of by past experience, but the slightest consideration proves how much he needs to be supported by the sympathy and prayers of the church.*

On his return to London, the first people he called on was Mrs. Weekes, who had taught him to read and write, and Admiral Leeke, the man who had rescued him from slavery in 1822. His gratitude to Henry Venn was unbounded and he instructed his children to always refer to him as, *'The Good Father of Africa.'*

On July 9, Adjai went to Oxford where, at a special Convocation, he was conferred with the Honorary Degree of Doctor of Divinity. In the minutes of the Register of the Hebdomadac Council of the University is recorded the confirmation of the degree.

But, soon after he was made a bishop he had to contend with the racism, which had started to rear its ugly head even before he was to reach this, one of the highest positions in the Anglican Church. Many of the white Anglicans resented his elevation and believed that his appointment was a mistake. As the 'Record' mentioned,*'the taunts of certain professors who maintain that the cerebral development of the Negro, show that he is disqualified for intellectual pursuits.'* They felt that the power the position as bishop gave him should not be held by a black person, but by a white person. Many of the white missionaries held the impression that the reigns of power should be held in white hands and did not like both African culture and the African's capacity to hold such a high office in what was a predominantly a white Christian religion. Perhaps, unbeknown to Adjai, he had several rivals and critics within the church, who objected to his elevation. One of these was the Rev. Henry Townsend with whom he had worked so closely to establish the mission and church in Abeokuta.

Although he thought he knew Townsend well, Adjai did not realise how much of a racist he was, and how envious he was of him and the ascendency of this African clergyman. His racist views are clearly stated in letters he wrote to Henry Venn, and in one dated 1851 he states:

'I have great doubt of young black clergymen. They want years of experience to give stability to their character; we would rather have them as schoolmasters and catechists'.

And in another in 1859 he wrote to Venn:

'It appears you intend to work up the native clergy to notice by sending with them inferior white men, but it won't answer. The white man must be in advance ability, in religion, in position to the native teachers of all kinds, or if he ceases to be so, he must leave the work.'

Three months later, he added:

'If you want young men to go to the Niger, you must give them a white man as leader. No opinion you can form, no statement you can make, no advice you can give will make them (i.e black men) what they are not. They are not fit to be leaders, at present'.

He was not the only racist within the Anglican church. The missionary at Ibadan, David Hinderer, when asked if he would be willing to place himself under a black bishop such as Adjai, had replied:

'*Not that I should have the slightest objection to Bishop Crowther being over myself and the congregation which God may give me. On the contrary, I can only respect and love him. But, the country is heathen and mixed up with and held up by heathen priest craft and we are allowed to teach and preach the Gospel, not because they are tired of heathenism, but because God gives us to influence as Europeans among them. This influence is very desirable and necessary if they hear that a black man is our master, they will question our respectability.*'

Even in 1864, still a racist Townsend wrote to a Methodist friend Thomas Champness, '*We are gone down so low that I am obliged to beg permission of Mr Maser (a missionary) to come here. How different to the time when a white face was a sufficient passport here.*'

Surprisingly for a Christian man who spent most of his working life amongst them, Townsend was not wholehearted enamoured with his African colleagues, and took every opportunity to disparage them. He had his most vitriolic comments against Adjai, of whom one can only imagine, he was envious.

These were some of the incidents of racism that the present Archbishop of Canterbury Justin

Welby, highlighted in his sermon to apologies for the behaviour of certain elements in the Church of England and the ill-treatment of Adjai. As stated earlier, he was preaching at the ceremony of 'thanksgiving and repentance' which was held in Canterbury Cathedral on the 4 June, 2014 to mark the one hundred and fifty years of the consecration of Samuel Adjai Crowther, as the first black bishop in the Anglican church. He said, *'This is a service of thanksgiving and repentance. Thanksgiving for the extraordinary life which we commemorate, and repentance, shame and sorrow for the Anglicans who are reminded of the sin of many of our ancestors. We, in the Church of England, need to say sorry that someone who was properly and rightly consecrated Bishop was then betrayed and let down. It was wrong'* he went on to say, *'But despite his passion and high achievement, Bishop Crowther's mission was undermined and dismantled in 1880 by racist white Europeans, including fellow missionaries. Historians said prejudiced fellow Anglican missionaries wrongly questioned the moral values and competency of Bishop Crowther and his African staff, and systemically dismantled his work. In the end he resigned.'*

Archbishop Welby quoted researchers from Boston University's School of Theology in the US who found, *'Mission policy, racial attitudes and evangelical spirituality had taken new directions and new source of European missionaries were now available. By degrees, Crowther's mission was dismantled: by financial controls, by young Europeans taking over, by dismissing, suspending, or transferring the African staff. Crowther, desolated resigned and died soon after of a stroke. He was replaced by a white bishop.'* RIP

In 1877 the CMS, acting on unfounded rumours about the mission stations under Adjai in West Africa, including the statements that the African clergymen 'were lazy, drunken and dissolute' appointed a lay European worker, which limited his powers and authority. So, gradually the African missionaries were replaced by Europeans, and by 1890 the Anglican Church in West Africa was once again in the hands of Europeans. It was not until **1952 before another black bishop was consecrated to lead the flock in West Africa.**

But, Adjai had many supporters such as Henry Venn and Thomas Fowell Buxton, who were both open minded and far sighted looking, who felt that the Gospel can, and should, be spread by Africans as well as Europeans. They were vocal in their support of Adjai. Venn saw in him the potential to demonstrate his idea of self-governing, self-supporting and self-propagating the African churches. And it was this move towards an Anglican version of the 'three self' formula that he pushed for Adjai to be consecrated as *'Bishop of the countries of Western Africa beyond the Queen's dominion.'*

I was struck that whilst researching his life for this book, I could not find any references to whether Adjai was aware of this racism swelling around him. If he was aware of it, he never mentioned it in any of his letters, or in his journals.

But, all this was to come later in his life. For, Adjai was strong in his faith and true to his God and persevered in his work to spread the gospel amongst his people. So, on July 24, he sailed on the *'Macgregor Laird'* for Sierra Leone arriving on August 4. Of course, news of his elevation reached Freetown even before he did and how proud his wife, family and the whole nation were to welcome him when he landed and to give him an enthusiastic welcome. They were pleased that a man of their own, a Yoruba man, had been elevated to the highest position in the Anglican church. He was returning to them as the first, and for many years, the only black Bishop in the whole of West Africa.

The day after his arrival, they organised an official welcome, which took place at Fourah Bay Institute, the very place where he had been educated and where he had been a teacher. There assembled clergy, catechists, missionaries, teachers and students and some of the great, good and influential people of Freetown, including the Governor, gathered to express their congratulations, gratitude and great joy at his elevation. Two addresses were read, signed and handed to him. One was by the whole body of the Church Missionary agents and native pastors, and the other by the Fourah Bay Institute authorities, for the great honour he had brought to his Alma Mater. The rather flowery first address, had over thirty-two signatures, and said in part, *'We regard your consecration as a token of God's favour to the church in Africa, and would unfeignedly rejoice with you in this mark of His distinguishing love, believing it, as we do, to be an earnest of richer blessings which are yet in store. In reviewing your own past career in this colony, and subsequently in Abeokuta and the Niger, we thank God for the abundant grace bestowed upon you and for the measure of success granted you in your missionary work, and we trust that the same grace may be vouchsafe to guide and comfort, to strengthen and support you through all your future course in the high office to which you have been called. It will be a source of comfort to you to know that prayer-meetings were held in the colony on the day of your leaving England that God would protect you from the dangers of the deep and you may rest assured that prayer will constantly ascend, that under your wise and judicious culture the thorn and thistle may be uprooted and the Rose of Sharon and the Lily of the Valley may be seen along the banks of the Niger. May the spirit of the Lord rest upon you, the spirit of wisdom and understanding making you as a chief pastor of the flock of Christ in Africa, of quick understanding in the fear of the Lord, so that you will judge not after the sight of your eyes, nor reprove after the hearing of your ears, but ruling and superintending all things according to truth and love.'*

Trying to hide his emotions, Adjai thanked them for their loving and sincere expressions towards him, and said, *'When we look back on the commencement we find the mission took its beginning from a heterogeneous mass of people, brought together in the providence of God from many tribes of this part of Africa, out of whom, through the zealous, faithful and persevering labour of the early missionaries, arose devout congregations of faithful and sincere Christians. After a time the mission produced a native ministry, the a self-supporting native pastorate, and latterly, out of the native ministry, an humble step outwards was taken in faith to introduce a native episcopate in mission beyond Her Majesty's dominions.' Here we pause and raise our Ebenezer to God's praise. Hitherto our Lord has helped us.*

This onward progress seems to be an indication from God, beckoning us to come forward, put our shoulder to the wheels and ease our European brethren of great work, which they have so nobly sustained alone from their predecessors for fifty years, many of whom had sealed the testimony of their zeal with their lives. Their graves at the burial grounds are existing monuments of their faithful obedience to their Master's command: "Go and teach all nations."

Whether called to their rest or whether beaten back from the fields of their labour through ill-health and forced to retire, or whether still labouring among us, it is our bounden duty in gratitude to remember and esteem them highly in love for their works sake, of which we are the fruits.

We must exhibit a missionary spirit ourselves, and encourage it among our congregation, if we are imitators of missionary enterprises; if, like as Timothy knew Paul, we also have known their zeal, we should endeavour to preach the Gospel in the regions beyond the colony. To extend our line of usefulness we must seriously impress on our Christian countrymen the necessity of exhibiting a spirit of liberality, after the example of the mother Church, whose spirit we should imbibe, not only to support their own pastors and school teachers, keeping in good repair their churches and other buildings made over into their hands, but also contribute, according to the means God has blessed them with, to send the Gospel into countries beyond them which are yet destitute of the blessings of its light.

But, above all, we must be followers of Christ, the Great Shepherd of His flock and the example of His apostles, in the habit of prayer for help from above. This is the weapon which prevails most in the work of the ministry. When we feel our weakness and insufficiency for the work to which God has called us, we must constantly go to the Throne of Grace for divine aid. We are better fitted when we feel our incompetency to change a sinner's heart. This will drive us to apply to the Fountain Head for a quickening spirit from above, which He has promised to all who ask Him; then we shall be encouraged to go on in this our might. Has he not sent you?'

The address from his Alma Mater said, 'We thank God for the grace bestowed on you, enabling you to labour so faithfully for the past thirty- five year in His service. This institution at one time enjoyed the benefit of your instruction, *but of late years the Yoruba and the Niger missions have been the fields in which you have laboured. Notwithstanding this, we have not been unmindful of you; your name has been familiar as a "household word" among us, and you have been held up as an example to our youth.'*

That Sunday he preached his first sermon as a Bishop, in Yoruba to a large crowd of his countrymen, who had gathered to hear the first black bishop. But, although he was destined to return to Abeokuta, yet his prolonged stay in Freetown gave him the opportunity to preach regularly in churches to large crowds which gathered to hear him. He sometimes preached in English and more times than not, in Yoruba. But, again sometimes in a mixture of both languages. Before he left Sierra Leone, he organised a missionary meeting at which he explained the work of the mission in Nigeria with a view to encourage some to join him.

Soon, he returned to Nigeria to begin work to strengthen the work of the mission and to train more local missionaries. Mrs. Crowther and the children were with him, and during their transit in Lagos, he was able to show his wife the very spot from which he had been taken aboard the ship in 1822 that was the beginning of his long journey to Christianity. As they walked about the area where it all began, he writes that he took off his hat and reverently thanked God. He later wrote, *'I could well recollect many places I knew during my captivity, so I went over the same spots where slave barracoons used to be. What a difference. Some of the spots are now converted into plantations of maize or cassava, and sheds built on others are filled with casks of palm oil and other merchandise, instead of slaves in chains and irons, in agony and despair.'*

While in Lagos he conducted his very first ordination service as a bishop, when he admitted a Mr Lambert Mackenzie to the deacon order.

One can only imagine the welcome he received when he eventually reached Abeokuta, the first black bishop to set foot in the town. He was welcomed by the chief, the people and the missionaries, and preached and administered the sacrament to hundreds of people. He was pleased with the progress of the evangelical work that had taken place while he was away.

Soon after his return, he was on his way again, this time hitching a ride on the *'Investigator'* and went up the Niger. For he was putting into practice what he had been consecrated to do, to visit the wide diocese beyond the limits of our dominions. With renewed energy he went up the Niger and its tributaries, something that another European would not have been able to do. He was a little man with nerves of steel and a constitution to march. Reaching Onitsha he held his second ordination before a crowd that looked on with wonder, at this strange ritual being performed by one of their own people. In his journal Adjai recoded his thoughts. *The native converts did not fully understand what it was, but entered our mission party entered into it with heart and soul. There was nothing grand in it, but a peculiar solemnity pervaded the whole service. The place of ordination, the congregation among whom it took place, the candidate for ordination, the assisting priest, and the officiating bishop, presenting such a novel scene, as if a new thing was taking place in Africa. Can this be real? Is this the way Christianity spread to remote countries in the first century of its promulgation? In the nineteenth century, the time 'when many shall run to and fro, and the knowledge shall be increased. When the wilderness and solitary place shall be glad for them and the desert shall rejoice and blossom as the rose.'*

He held a confirmation of five settlers from Sierra Leone at Ghebe, which was a new occasion for the people who flocked to witness the ceremony. He afterward administered the Sacrament and baptised ten adults and seven children.

He went to Bonny in the eastern part of Nigeria, and founded the first Delta mission station there. For King Peppel of the Delta area, who had made a visit to England in 1860, had petitioned the Bishop of London to send missionaries to his area to spread the Christian gospel. When Adjai arrived in the area, he had great difficulty locating a suitable place in which to set up the mission. But he eventually did, and the small mission church of St. Peters was inaugurated on the 1 January, 1872. He established churches and missions in Onitsha and Lokoja in 1857, Akassa at the mouth of river Niger in1861, Bonny in 1864 and Brass in 1868. Wherever he set up his missions, trade and commerce soon followed, and in doing so helped to stop the slave trade, of which he was once the byproduct.

But, all was not plain sailing for the Bishop in spreading the word of God amongst a people who for centuries had been steeped in superstition and cannibalism. In fact, Bonny had the reputation of cannibalism being a common practice, with human sacrifices being offered at the death of a chief. Juju and fetish temples abounded in the place, where scenes of revolting practices took place. But to this place of such barbarity and cruelty Adjai was to bring the Gospel of the Lord. Succeeded he did, due to the King William Peppel and the other chiefs, who cordially welcomed him and signed agreements for the establishment of the mission. And against all objections from the people, the place chosen to build the mission was at a place that the people thought was a place they had used to bury the bodies of people who had been scarified and left to die. Building a mission on such land, the people felt, would make their gods angry and visit great palaver on them. But the Bishop was not to be put off. He said, *'Give us the land and leave us and the juju to settle the palaver.'* But he had great difficulty getting the people to help clear the land, and even to go near the place. But, the King sent his son and ten men to clear the land and the mission house was built.   But, not before the young prince had asked the Bishop to read a portion of the scriptures and pray and bless the land, before he and his men could start the work.

The church building was soon completed with its crowning feature being a great bell, which had been laying around since 1824. It was inscribed with the words, *William Dobson, founder, Downham, Norfolk, England.* This bell was cast for Opooboo

Foobra, King of Grand Bonny, in the year 1824. No one seemed to know how this great bell reached this remote part of the Niger in the first place, but it came in useful to grace the new church in Bonny. So, on Easter Day 1867, to much fanfare, the Gospel was preached for the first time and the King and people of Bonny, renounced the worship of the monitor lizard or iguana, and accepted the worship of the true God. To see what hold the worship of these creatures had on the superstition on the people of Bonny, here we must print part of a lecture by Sir H. H. Johnston, he gave to the Royal Geographical Society in London, when he pointed out that the animal worship was so real in Bonny at the time, that the British authorities on the river was compelled to afford it a certain recognition. In his lecture he says:

'At Bonny, the monitor lizards became a sickening nuisance. They devour the European's fowls, turkeys, ducks and geese with impunity; they might lie across the road or the doorways of houses with their six feet of length and savagely lash the shins of the people who attempted to pass them with their whip-like serrated tails, and if you wounded, or killed one of them there was no end of a to-do. You were assaulted, or robbed by the natives, harangued by the consul on board of a man-of-war, and possibly fined into the bargain. For its effectual abolishment, which has been of the greatest benefit to the well-being of the Europeans and natives alike, we owe our thanks, not to the intervention of the naval and consular officials, nor to the bluff remonstrations of traders, but to the quiet, unceasing labours of

Bishop Samuel Crowther and the agents of the Church Missionary Society.'

But here let the Bishop himself tell the story of the extirpation of these privileged pests:

'22 April,1867. You will be glad to hear that yesterday, at the mutual consent of myself and chiefs, the geedee or guana, Bonny juju, was declared to be no longer Bonny juju, and many of the townsmen are killing them.

No sooner was this renunciation made and orders given to clear the town of them than many persons turned out in pursuit of these poor reptiles, which had been so long idolised, and now kill them as if it were in revenge, and strew their carcass all about in open places and markets by the dozen and scores; fifty-seven were counted at one marketplace where they were exposed to public view as proof of the people's conviction and former error, and that they were determined to reform in good earnest in this respect. Everywhere one went the carcasses of the guana met the sight. There was another decision made respecting the removal of the guanas. Lest they should hereafter say he had not had some share in the extinction of the sacred reptiles, it was decided that some of the blood should be sprinkled into all the wells of Bonny town to indicate that they had concurred not only with the destruction, but also with its use as food. Many soon began to feed upon the flesh, roasted with fire. This reminds me of the passage "And he took the calf which they had made, and burnt it in the fire, and ground it to powder and strewed it upon the water, and made the children of Israel drink it." (Exodus xxxii.20)'

The Bishop had such an effect on the King and the people of Bonny that when he died his son wrote to inform him of his death:

'His life has been one of the most extraordinary and remarkable kind for an African king. He was King in 1855 at the age of nineteen, and after reigning between nineteen and twenty years he had a misunderstanding with the chiefs, which made him go to Fernando Po, from thence to the Island of Ascension, and from thence to London, where he landed in June,1856, and resided there until June 1861, when he set sail for his native land, arriving in Bonny in August, and by God's grace again ascended his rightful throne. Having seen England and having had even before his visit a wish to bring the missionaries into his dominion, he instructed me to write to the Bishop of London, who handed over the letter to you, which made you visit Bonny in 1864, and the agreement was drawn. The rest you know and I need not repeat it. I am glad to hear of your prosperous visit to and return from the Niger, and that the kings of the different countries down that river are upholding and introducing Christianity in their countries thanks to you. As for me, the work which my father began, with your help, I will never deny or desert.'

It was not all good sailing for the work of the new bishop and from time to time there were set - backs. For example, the work he had striven so hard to set up in Ghebe where he had conducted his second ordination after becoming bishop, came under sustained attack. This was a place where several tribes from all parts met: the Igbara, Yoruba, Igara, Nupe, Kakanda, Doma and Djuka and came together to trade. One day, news reached the bishop that the town had been destroyed and its mission put to the torch. One of those infrequent tribal wars had broken out with little warning and during the battle the men at Ghebe had been defeated and the town burned to the ground. The British consul, Mr Fell had been able to protect some of the Christians, but many had been killed. The Bishop made haste to visit the town in order to bring some peace between the warring tribes, and confronted the chiefs. In his journal he records:

'I made a point to show them what they were doing to themselves and the people at large; that God had brought the way of peace to them, but they have chosen war; God had brought blessing and prosperity to them, but they have abused it and did not appreciate these things; that they have deprived Ghebe, our first station at the Confluence, of all the advantages it had above all other places - the privilege of the place of worship, of civilisation and industry and trade, all of which we introduced at great expenses for the general good of the country; but, they regarded them not. How could they expect to prosper under such circumstances? This lecturing must have had some effect as the bishop retired as he says leaving both parties under the deep impression of their misdoings and consequences.'

In Onitsha someone set fire to some dry grass, and the wind blew it in the direction of the mission building. The building was soon raised to the ground, but luckily with no loss of life.

Although Abeokuta was not strictly part of the Niger mission, yet it was close to the heart of the bishop for it was there that he set up the first Christian mission in Nigeria 'under the stone.' So, any problems that occurred in Abeokuta. Mr. Townsend, the missionary in whom they had put so much trust, had returned to England for health reasons. With no one to mediate between the Christians and the non-Christians, things went from bad to worse. The Christians were continually being harassed by the King Gezo of Dahomey who waged war on the areas around Abeokuta, capturing and selling slaves. He was a bloodthirsty demagogue, who committed great cruelty on any who fell into his hands. On Sunday 13 October, 1867 the town crier went around the town prohibiting anyone from attending churches, or Sunday school. But, in spite of this the Christians of several denominations such as the Wesleyan, Baptist and the Church of England Society, defied the call and attended their places of worship. They were attacked and beaten, the premises were looted and destroyed, and the missionaries were told to leave the town at once. So the missionaries and the Christian converts, a forlorn and pity group, left their plundered houses and ruined churches behind and slowly left Abeokuta. So all the work that Adjai had put into setting up the Christian mission in Abeokuta was destroyed overnight.

CHAPTER 10
KIDNAPPED, CAPTURED AND
RESCUED AGAIN

But, the Bishop himself was not to escape the indignity of being held prisoner, for he was kidnapped and held prisoner for twenty-eight days with his son Dandeson and only escaped by the skin of his teeth. He and his son Dandeson had been tricked by Abokko, a chief he considered to be friend. He was on one of his trips on the Niger on his missionary journeys in September, 1867 when he put in at a place called Oko-Okien, which was where the chief had stationed himself. When Adjai met the chief, he noticed that he had a cross expression on his face, and being old friends Adjai greeted him in the usual way, but his greeting was repulsed and he sensed that something was wrong. The chief asked where was his presents and Adjai said what presents? While they were exchanging words, Adjai noticed that the some of the village men had rushed to his boat and apprehended his boatmen and put them in chains, and were plundering the boat. He ordered his son, who was in the boat, to leave the boat and allow the men to plunder as much as they wanted to. The boat was stripped of everything, masts and sails and then taken up the creek.

The chief took everything they had, including their personal belongings and vestments and surplices, papers, books, bedding, the provision box, fifty pounds in gold and silver coins intended to pay the salaries of the agents in Lokoja and 16,000 cowries to buy provisions. As usual, Adjai kept a detailed account in his private diary and it is from this that we hear from his own words what happened during his kidnap and captivity. He writes:

'When he tired, I took the opportunity of his quietness and addressed him, "Abokko, what was my offence that you serve me so strangely today?" He replied, "You have committed no offence whatever." I replied that if I had committed no offence I could not account for his hostility towards me, in seizing my boat and plundering all my luggage in such an unexpected manner, especially when I put in to pay him my respects as a friend. Then Abokko poured forth a long stream of complaints which had moved him to act.

That he, although superintendent of the board of trade in this part of the river, was not recognised by the English merchants; that he was slighted by being made only small and paltry presents, unworthy of his high rank; neither would the ships open trade with him; that he went on board last year, as also this year, but they would not trade with him.

That three ships had visited the river this year (taking the Thomas Bazeley's two trips as to be two different ships) yet none would recognise him. Although the small ship, Investigator, stopped at Idda and gave handsome presents to the Atta, yet he who owns the river and all the Oibos who travel on it was contemptuously overlooked; that as I knew all things about him, I ought to have represented him to the gentlemen of the ship's property; that as I had not done so he would not let me go till such a time as large presents were given him and trade opened with him.

No explanation I could give would satisfy Abokko. In vain I assured him that it was beyond my power to control trading affairs or arrange with other departments what presents to give or where or with whom to trade. Abokko said he knew well that I possessed the establishments at Lokoja, Idda, Onitsha, Bonny, etc., and he believed that I owned the ships and also could direct them as I pleased. All my attempts to explain to Abokko the wide difference between mission stations and trading merchants were of no avail. He demanded three boat loads of goods for each of the three ships to effect my release. I referred him to Idda station, where there is not as yet a trading establishment, as a specimen of my other stations at Lokja and Onitsha. In that station I saw no traffic going on but the simplicity of missionary work, but that would not satisfy him.

That night came on and no impression could be made upon Abokko to change his tone, or soften his treatment. He sent me and a party to take our quarters in an open shed, occupied by his canoe boys, on a mat laid on the damp ground, which served us for a bed for the night, without a morsel even of yams or corn to satisfy the cravings of nature. I sent to ask for some of my own yams, which had been plundered in the boat, but Abokko said he was not aware before that Oibos were in the habit of eating late in the *evening and so we had to go without. We passed the night just as we jumped out of the boat; one of Abokko's slaves, pitying our condition, offered me his country cloth for covering. I admired his tender feelings and self-denial thanked him, and begged him to keep it for his own use. One of our boatmen took off his tobe and gave it to me for a pillow, as he had another cloth to cover himself with. I accepted it for Dandeson, whose head was on bare ground, I having a small raised earth under my head, softened with my cap. Thus, we passed the night; I need not say sleeplessly, for my thoughts were full of those unexpected trials and the difficult situation into which I so ignorantly and innocently walked, without the least apprehension of treachery from such a quarter. But, the God of mercies will interpose. Since my detention here I have been told that Abokko had planned to attack the 'Thomas Bazeley' while she was aground in the neighbourhood, but could not carry it out for want of men to support him.'*

The Bishop and his son Dandeson and Mr. Moore, the bricklayer who was travelling with them, had to endure nine days of the whims of Abokko before they were rescued. During their enforced stay at the mercy of the wicked Abokko, Dandeson celebrated his twenty-fourth birthday, not amongst his siblings and friends but in a shed on the banks of the Niger. As the bishop recorded on 24 September:

'Far away as he was from home and relatives, except myself and friends and from all comforts, my wishes for him on this occasion were

that he might be permitted to see many a return of the day, to which this of his captivity in his first career of missionary life might be the beginning of a new era. We are thankful that what has befallen us met us in the path of duty in our Master's cause.'

The plight of the kidnap and detention of the bishop and party had not gone unnoticed, and the King of Atta sent his messenger to Abokko to find out what was happening. Having ascertained that the bishop had been held captive and his boat plundered, the messenger returned to inform the king what had taken place. No sooner had he left than a messenger called Abbega, arrived from the Consul in Lokoja. He brought an encouraging letter for the bishop, and some presents and a letter requesting Abokko to release the bishop and party to return with him to Lokoja. Abokko point blank refused, and after a long parley with the messenger, he agreed to release them for one thousand bags of cowries, equivalent to £1000 on the Niger, for the bishop and the same for his son. The mediator over-ruled this, and he settled for that sum for the release of the whole party. This amount he wanted paid in coral beads, velvets, white satins, and cowries.

The Bishop wrote a letter to the consul, which Abbega was to take with him the following day, Tuesday 1 October. It was then proposed that Dandeson and Mr. Moore should go to Lokoja with Abbega in order to lighten the load, but Dandeson refused to leave his father behind and so, Mr. Moore went with Abbega to Lokoja. As soon as they left, writing in his journal this is what the Bishop wrote:

'Sept 28. The 'Thomas Bezeley' very unexpectedly arrived early this morning with W. Fell, Esq. under the consul's flag, having met Abbega on the way with my letter to the consul and anchored opposite the village. Mr Fell landed, accompanied by W. V. Rolleston, Esq., late of the 22 West Indian Regiment, being passenger on board, together with my two sons, Abbega, and some of Masaba's men. They immediately communicated with me, and told me their already prearranged plan to take us away without paying anything for our release. I advised that Mr. Fell should see Abokko and hear for himself what he really wanted, that he might satisfy himself as regards the price charged; at the same time to assure the chief that I have no influence over the merchants, the chiefs, or trading affairs, my simple business being to teach the people God's Book, in which work I was engaged when he seized my boat, plundered my luggage and detained me.'

Mr. Fell did so, but Abokko was adamant that the bishop would not take one step away without the payment. As he argued with the king, he urged the bishop to run for the boat which he did and amidst all the confusion, made it and the boat pulled away to the ship. Amidst a hail of musket fire from the shore and shots of poisoned arrow, and fire cover from the ship, they made it to the ship. But, not before Mr. Fell had received a mortal wound from a poisoned arrow. The ship weighed anchor immediately and was away from the village. But sadly, Mr. Fell who had risked his life to save the bishop, expired just before they reached Lokoja. The bishop was very heartbroken, as he recorded in his journal:

'It would have been satisfactory to me, had such been the will of God, had I been shot and my dead body taken to Lokoja instead of his. But Mr Fell had acted gallantly, zealously, and praiseworthy in his determination never to lower the honest character of British merchant by paying a covetous rebel the sum of £1000 to encourage a treacherous breach of confidence, friendship and hospitality. I have never shrank from the pursuit of my duty from mere personal exposure to dangers common to all travellers by land, or by water, but I never expected such treachery from a professed friend; against this I could not guard.'

The Bishop never forgot to thank the people who had saved him from a fate worse than death. In a letter of thanks to Colonel Rolleston for the part he played in his rescue, he states:

'Permit me to express my feelings of unfeigned gratitude for your kind and active assistance, rendered to deliver us out of treacherous Abokko at Oke-Okein. The more I think of your succour, covering me with your person, and hastening me into the boat to our middle water, the greater obligation I shall ever feel for the sacrifice you had made by thus defending me; you exposed yourself to personal dangers such as had happened, to my great

regret, to our much lamented friend, Mr. W. Fell. Had you not from pity acted in such a decided manner, in all probability our liberation would have been long delayed, and the Committee of the Church Missionary Society would have been left in long and anxious suspense as to what has become to us in the hand of the piratical Abokko, unless the amount charged was paid.

May your life be long spared, and in God's all-wise Providence you may be an instrument, directly or indirectly, by devising plans, to do much good for the improvement of the tribes of these large and populous parts of Africa.'

The children of the Bishop were also very grateful for the rescue of their father by Mr. Rolleston, that Abgail, the daughter who was married to the Rev. T. B. Macauley, wrote to Mrs. Rolleston to express their gratitude. In the letter dated 16 November, 1867 from the Lagos Grammar School, she writes:

'Dear Mrs. Rolleston,

I would not have taken the liberty of writing to you, being a perfect stranger, had I not been asked to do so by your dear husband, to accompany a few trifles I send to your dear children. I trust Mr. Rolleston has reached you safely and mentioned to you the invaluable service he has done for our family in the rescue of our dear father from the hands of wicked Abokko. Mr. Rolleston's name is immortalised in our family, and is mentioned every day. I send you one of my bracelets as a curiosity and all to put you in mind of the same even. It is the palm nut carved, and may have got discoloured before it reached you; a little oil rubbed on will give its black colour again. Trusting you are enjoying good health with your family and with respects to Mr. Rolleston and yourself.

I am, dear Mrs. Rolleston,
yours respectfully
Abigail Crowther Macaulay'

Much later, it was discovered that the kidnapping had been arranged between the Atta and Abokko, as some of the looted goods such as the Bishop's tea-kettle, a pair of elastic-sided boots and a cup, clearly belonging to the Bishop and his party, were found in the possession of the Atta. He had arranged to split the £1000 ransom with Abokko. When this treachery was discovered, it was decided to abandon the mission station without much delay, and the mission workers and their wives and children hastily got on board the '*Thomas Bazeley*' leaving behind their furniture, books and belongings. This is what the Atta was waiting for, and he seized the spoils. So with much sorrow, the mission station at Idda was relinquished, much to the regret of the Bishop.

The native pastors at Lokoja, in expressing their sympathy with the Bishop at his detention by Abokko, together with both heathen, Mohammedans and Christians wrote to the Bishop saying:

'Be assured, Right Rev. and dear Sir, that in your suffering fervent prayers were offered up at the throne of Grace on your behalf, and none

were more glad than we in observing that our prayers had not been in vain. We are hereby encouraged in our reliance on the promises of God; "When thou passest through the waters, I will be with thee: when thou walkest through fire, thou shalt not be burned; neither shall the flame kindle upon thee." In your patient endeavour of the distress in which you were placed we have a bright example of suffering all things for Christ's sake, and whenever we are called upon to suffer any like calamity for the Cross of Christ our Master we shall inevitably think of your sufferings and take courage. And oh, may we have the measure of grace which has hitherto characterised your deportment under the most painful circumstances. And we do not fail here to convey our sympathy also with your dutiful son, who, though young and unaccustomed to privations, yet braved them when called to do so in order that you might not be too anxious for his sake, and so add sorrow upon sorrow.'

The greatest challenges faced by the Bishop in bringing the word of God to his people were paganism and the entrenched pagan traditions of the people. For Christianity dealt a blow to ancestral worship, witchcraft, traditional gods and the entrenched institution of polygamy. In trying to convert the people to the true way, the Bishop came across resistance from the chiefs and kings and the juju men, who called the wrath of their gods on all who converted, and this created a raft of divisions between converts and non converts. But, the biggest headaches suffered initially was polygamy. The question of Christian marriage versus polygamy was one that the church had to grapple with for a long time.

It is said, Bishop Crowther maintained that he approached the question of polygamy as he approached slavery, namely to demand from converts seeking baptism no more than the minimum qualification necessary for salvation. He did not interfere with local customs and practices which Christianity after a time will abolish.

He was sternly rebuked by Henry Venn, the Secretary of the Church Missionary Society, who argued that Christ regarded polygamy as adultery, and whatever be the prevalent customs of a nation, the ordinance of God could not be lowered to it, there must be one standard for the church everywhere, as God could not condemn polygamy, in an old-established Church and accept it in a new way. This was a public putdown and, according to (Adjai 1965 page 106,) the Bishop shut up and even recounted saying, *'I have never at any time had a doubt in my mind as to the sinfulness of polygamy, and as contrary to God's holy ordinance from the creation and confirmed in the time of the flood.'* It is interesting to note that when the memorandum came up for discussion at the 1888 Lambeth Bishop Crowther was one of its stout defenders.

According to Adjai, the Bishop's son, Archdeacon Dandeson Crowther, even went further. He said that he had no problem with the fate of wives who had been in a polygamous marriage and had been divorced, seeking baptism, because such wives were not wives, but slaves.

The Bishop was torn between what he knew was happening among his flock and what the bible says about polygamy. Fearlessly he grappled with the subject as he addressed his pastors.

'Many would place it prominently above all obstacles in the way of Christian missions in Africa, but perhaps I do not go to the same extent as they do ranking it as the greatest hindrance embracing Christianity, though it is the most common. The system prevails throughout the country; it insinuates itself into the corrupt and unsubdued will of the children of Adam. It has enslaved the female population and made many to be miserable victims to the cruel lust and depraved appetite of one man. It has wrenched from them the right of nature which God has implanted in each for their own social happiness. Let us stand above the level and take a view of this social evil. It is impossible for every polygamist in this country to support from two to half a dozen wives out of his own scanty resources, and when this is the case there is no alternative but, that every wife must enter into a life of labour and drudgery and shift for herself the best way she can. Hence, to earn her own livelihood, she must become a carrier of loads from one market town to another, or she must be a trader to neighbouring town and tribes, which involves an absence of days and weeks and months from home and on her return it has not infrequently happened that she provides for the husband out of her earnings in addition to providing for herself and her children, if she has any, for the chief care of the children devolves on *the mother and her relatives. It has been remarked by the men themselves that when a man has but one wife, there was that degree of love and affection between them as might be observed in a married state in civilised countries - they were one in everything. But, no sooner that a second wife is added than the cord of union and affection was broken and the domestic evils immediately showed themselves. Thence arose this memorable proverb among the Yoruba females 'No woman would ever undergo the expenses of a sacrifice to procure a rival.' That is that her husband may have an additional wife. The proverb is their own; it is their watchword, showing the repugnance of their feelings against the system. But it is normally suppressed like their other proper rights, which they forgo for fear of being reproached with jealousy.*

He quotes one of the obstacles that the missionaries face when it comes to the question of polygamy, which is from the writings of Captain Richard Burton, who writes in his book on ABEOKUTA AND THE CAMEROONS:

'"Polygamy is the foundation-stone of Yoruba society. I can assure the missionaries that had less objection been made to polygamy on their part, the heathen would have found fewer obstacles to conversion. Those who hold it their duty to save souls should seriously consider whether they are justified in placing such stumbling blocks upon the path of improvement." Whether one should take Richard Burton as the truth or not, but what he says is not far from the

truth as he did live amongst the primitive peoples in various parts of Africa and studied and some say, took part in some of their primitive sexual rituals. So he must know what he was writing about.'

The Bishop went on to say that It has been suggested by some that the present polygamists could be received into the church by the Sacrament of baptism, on condition that such persons promise not to add to their already possessed wives; but who can guarantee that young persons will not purposely hold back till they have possessed as many wives as their hearts desire before they offer themselves to be admitted into the church by the same rites as their fathers? The human heart is so deceitful and desperately wicked that it will ever find a loophole to gratify its carnal propensity. Once establish a precedent it cannot easily be changed.

But, it seems that the Bishop had some sympathy for women who found themselves in a polygamous marriage. For he asks, in his address to the pastors, **'What hinders the female population from a readier profession of the religion?'** Whether their husbands be polygamists or not, as long as a woman remains faithful to her husband, upon her profession in faith in Christ as the all-sufficient Saviour of sinners, after a course of instruction she is received into the church by baptism; her husband's fault cannot be imputed to her, and if her will were consulted she would rather be the only helpmate for him.

The son of the Bishop, Archdeacon Dandeson Crowther, also had a soft spot and sympathy for women who found themselves in a polygamous marriage. He is reported to have said that he had no problem with the fate of wives divorced by a polygamist seeking baptism. For he thinks that such wives are no wives at all in the sight of God, they are but slaves.

But the views of the Bishop about polygamy did not go down well with his masters in the CMS headquarters in Salisbury Square in London, where it was felt that Christ regarded polygamy as adultery. Later on the Bishop was to recant when he said I have never, at any time, had any doubt in my life that polygamy is sinful and is contrary to God's Holy ordinance from the creation and confirmed in the time of the flood.

Another more forceful obstacles to the missionary work in Nigeria, was the draw of the Muslim religion, which was very strong and widespread along the upper reaches of the river Niger. The Muslims seem to be able to make converts of the people than the Christians. Asked why this was so, the Bishop said that it was because the muslim religion finds the native mind in a fit state to receive its teachings. The muslims had made inroads into the country some two hundred years earlier, and made converts through slavery and wars. For the conquered were forced to become Muslims on pain of death. The only other alternative was to be sold and transported overseas. The Bishop got to know the workings of the Muslim leaders and how they went about recruiting their converts. They set up schools that were attended by both men and women and children, where they were given the koran wrapped in paper, as talisman to be tied about their necks and bodies. This was to give them luck either in their trading or, where women were concerned, to provide prosperity in their households. The people had such faith in these paper talisman that some even asked the Bishop to give them scraps of paper as good luck.

On the subject of how to deal with the Muslims, extracts from one of his letters give some ideas of how to deal with the Muslims. The first, sent to the Rev. Henry Venn from Fernando Po on 22 June, 1857 says:

'It is very useful to be exercised in Greek and Latin and, if possible, in Hebrew characters and inflections, but I think Arabic aught to have the first place in these classic studies. All our Muslim population with whom we come in daily contact, both in Sierra Leone, in Yoruba and up the Niger, have more or less knowledge of the use of Arabic characters. As our labours are now extending among this class of peoples, it is necessary that the ordained native missionaries should know also the use of these characters. It will have fresh effects to meet these Muslims with their own weapons, not so much by arguments and vexatious disputation, but by the Christian minister being able to point out from his Arabic bible the important truth of Christianity. Though they may not believe, yet they will be humbled at the superior knowledge of their own book.'

The powers that be in London must have heard the cry from the wilderness by the Bishop, because writing from Kipo Hill station some twenty-six years later in 1883, the Bishop states:

'There are two Arabic readers about the village who assume the title of priest, also attendants at Katsa, who listened attentively to the preaching of the Gospel; but, are not content with what they heard only, are desirous of reading the same from the Arabic bible at the station and have since attended the Sunday school for this purpose to read passages of the Scriptures; though they could not give a translation in the native language of what they read in Arabic, yet Mr Paul always gave them the correct translations into the native language.'

Some time, from 1875 onwards Adjai and his Niger mission came under increasing attacks from European missionaries of the CMS in London. They complained that his mission was not carried forward with enough energy, and many of the people he appointed, clergymen, laymen and agents were not competent enough, were lazy, dissolute and were living lives not worthy of their callings. Several agents were dismissed without his knowledge, and at one point in 1889 even Archdeacon Dandeson Crowther, his son, was himself threatened with dismissal, and Archdeacon Johnson was transferred from his post. But, the Europeans who were sent to take over were soon decimated by disease. There was so much interference from London and the debacle it created that after the resignation of Adjai, and soon after his death, his son Dandeson formed the Delta mission stations into an independent pastorate which broke off from CMS control, although it remained under the Anglican umbrella.

Here, one must pay some attention to the son who followed his father into the Anglican church. Dandeson Coates Crowther was the second son of Adjai and his wife Asano. He was born in Freetown in 1844 and was one of the foundation students at the Lagos Grammar School, which was started by his brother-in-law in 1860, the Rev. T. B. Macauley, who was married to his elder sister. He was sent to England to train at the CMS College Islington. He was ordained a Deacon at St. Mary's Church, Islington on the 10 June, 1870, and consecrated a priest by his father on 12 March, 1871. He was awarded the OBE for his lifetime work in the Anglican Church and died in Freetown in 1938.

It is rather difficult to shift fact from fiction as to what happened to the splendid work that Adjai had done for Christianity, and why there was so much opposition from European missionaries. This sad part of his work has been glossed over by many European writers and the few facts that one can glean have been quite confusing. But, one of the most informative and straight forward report about the last days of his legacy has been written by P. E. H. Hair in The Early Study Of Nigerian Languages: Essays and Bibliographies, published by Cambridge University Press. Between pages 88 and 89, he writes about the quantity and output of linguistic materials published when Adjai was in charge.

'The devotion of the Niger Mission to this work is apparent in Crowther's published reports and even more in the page of unpublished Niger correspondence in the C. M. S. Archives. Yet none of the members of the Niger Mission had a full

university training; most of them had attended only a West African secondary school, or the largely theological courses at Fourah Bay Institution and a fair number of them had attended only elementary school. Their educational attainments were, therefore, on the average inferior to those of the largely-European staff of the other missions. Moreover, the Niger Mission agents had been drawn from a small community of English-speaking West Africans - not more than30,000 - of whom less than half were literate; and in this Freetown community, at least by the 1870s, those who were the intellectual cream were aspiring after secular and more remunerative occupations in medicine and law. Crowther's staff were almost wholly men of no special intellectual distinction, by normal standard; they were a very ordinary set of men who in other circumstances would not have been expected to produce what they did. Indeed, one must go further and say that they had not even the normal advantage of contemporary men in Europe who grew up in a literate society. Many of the agents of the Niger mission had (it may be assumed) illiterate parents, and all grew up in a society the vastly majority of whose members were only introduced to literacy when in their middle years they were brought to Freetown. Regarded against this background, the linguistic work of the Niger mission was extraordinary and can be interpreted as a notable achievement of human endeavour'.

As can be seen, Adjai had to make use of the African men he had at his disposal. No European had been sent by the CMS to help him set up his missions and he had to do so single handed. As to the accusation that he recruited and employed only men from the Freetown community, one must realise that these were men with some education, however limited to only reaching elementary standards. At least they were literate and could read and write in English. The Colonial Government in later years, also recruited men from the Freetown community to serve as clerks and junior administrators in the Gold Coast and Nigeria, when those countries were being administered under colonial rule. Almost all the men who ran the Cable and Wireless stations along the coast as far as Luanda, were men recruited from Freetown. At one time, Freetown was known as 'the Athens' of West Africa as it produced all of the most educated people in West Africa. It had the first institute of higher learning in Fourah Bay Institute, later becoming a constituent college of Durham University, and presently a university. Fourah Bay was started in 1827 and until the middle of the last century, was the only institution of higher learning in the whole of West Africa, to which students from Nigeria, Ghana and the Gambia flocked for their university education. It must be said that Adjai, using his local knowledge and influence with the local chiefs, was able to set up missions stations in Bonny in 1864, Nembre in 1868, Elem Kalabari in 1874 and Okrika in 1880. In fact the chiefs of Bonny and Nembre invited the CMS to come and establish schools in their areas in order to teach their children to read, write and speak English for they realised the importance of the trade and commerce the benefits these would bring.

So, to criticise Adjai for employing men as agents and clergy from the Freetown community, *'whose educational attainment were therefore on the average inferior to those of the largely-European staff of the other missions'* does him a grave injustice. For between 1857 and 1893, over fifty books and booklets were published in the languages of the lower Niger-Benue, and almost all were produced by West Africans. All these research, translating, writing and academic activities were due to the Niger mission under the influence of Adjai. These were men he knew and could trust, who spoke the same language as himself, who respected and looked up to him, and were eager to learn from him. One could not call his own son, Dandeson 'illiterate'. He was an ordained priest, studied in England and eventually became an Archdeacon. In 1883 he came to England and purchased two new churches for the Brass River, paid for by the subscriptions by the local Christians. Made of iron, the churches were carried in different sections first by ship from England and by canoes to the spot where they were to be erected on the Brass River.

It is interesting to note that the 1910 World Missionary Conference, which was held in Edinburgh, Archdeacon Dandeson Crowther, son of Adjai, nor James Johnson, the Sierra Leonean who had been consecrated assistant bishop of Western Equatorial Africa in 1900, was invited to attend the meeting. These were the two most senior African clergy in the Anglican church, who with Adjai, had given their lives to work diligently and tirelessly, to spread the gospel in West Africa on behalf of the Church Missionary Society. They were marginalised as being 'not fit' to attend such an important and august gathering of white missionaries. Some writers have speculated that if the gathering had taken place twenty-five earlier, Adjai would certainly have received an invitation to attend, as it would have been his indubitable right as an Anglican bishop, to attend such an august gathering of the great and good in the missionary world. For after all, he had been at the first three Lambeth Conferences in 1867, 1878 and 1888 as was his right.

It was the 1880s and by then Adjai had laboured in the field for over sixty years in the service of the Church Missionary Society. His mentor and guardian Henry Venn, and passed on and the new man called Hutchinson, was now at the helm of that great worldwide charitable missionary institution, and was a different breed altogether. He brought about direct European supervision of Adjai and the work he had laboured all his life to set up and build. A European Lay worker, J. A. Robinson was sent out, in order to restrict his authority. And so, gradually, the Niger mission that had taken him over fifty years to start and setup, was being dismantled. With the advancement of medicine Europeans did not die as often as they had done before when sent to West Africa and they were soon replacing the 'native' clergy with their new ways of doing things, and one must add, their racist prejudices against the African. The trust and confidence between Adjai and the CMS at Salisbury Square in London, was gradually eroded and was soon lost under the new regime. One can only assume that Adjai, who was used to doing things the old way with the support of his mentor Henry Venn, was not happy at the new broom that was sweeping the CMS.

But, undaunted by the critical erosion of his authority, Adjai continued with this work, and even though he was in his seventies continued to visit the various mission stations along the Niger. In 1884 he was on a tour of the missions when he received word of the death of his mother. In a letter he wrote while on board the 'SS Qualaba' dated 6 February 1, 1884 he poured out of his feelings: *'During my absence up the Niger my aged mother has been called to rest at the advanced age of ninety-seven years. We have much cause to be thankful that she was spared to us so long in the midst of so many adverse changes in her cause of life and family circumstances, to be at last brought to know the Saviour in whom she placed her trust as her Good Shepherds to the end of her life. When after twenty-five years of separation through the violence of slave war, we were brought together again through God's good providence at Abeokuta in 1864. I told her then that she must not expect that I should be stationary at home with her as other members of the family would be, because I was a travelling public servant. Her reply was 'You are no longer my son, but the servant of God, whose work you must attend unto without any anxiety for me; it is enough that I am permitted to see you once more in this world. To this resolution she kept to the last.'*

When she was on her dying bed, she told Mrs .Macaulay, her granddaughter, who was attending her as follows: *"Iya (mother) warned me not to write to you and tell you of her state then, for fear of perplexing your mind; she said to me 'will you not tell him what took place afterwards? Are you afraid? I replied 'I am not afraid' then she said 'you are as good as your father being at home; keep near to me, you have a great work to do.'' This was the last account I received of her about me, when not many years after she entered into her everlasting rest. I state this that you may know what valued she placed on my missionary work among our heathen brethren.*

In the year 1887 a Mr J.A. Robinson was appointed by London to be secretary of the Niger Mission, based in Onitsha, with Adjai as its chairman. The clash between the two men of God, which had been simmering for a while, came to a head at a meeting in 1890, when Robinson tried to usurp the powers of the chairman over the clergy. **Not to let this pass, the proud Adjai tendered his resignation which, without hesitation, was accepted.** Archdeacon Dandeson Crowther, the son of Adjai, angry at the way his father had been treated, separated his church from CMS control, and founded a native Niger Delta Pastorate Church, even though his father tried to persuade him not to do so. This separation was to last for more than thirty years. The CMS did show signs of a reconciliation in 1891 with formal approval of the constitution as an independent church.

Preaching at the **'service of thanksgiving and repentance'** to mark the hundred and fifty years of the consecration of Adjai in June,2014, Archbishop Welby said, *'In spite of immense* hardship and despite the racism of many whites, he evangelised so effectively that he was eventually ordained Bishop, over protest. He led his missionary diocese brilliantly, but was in the end falsely accused and had to resign, not long before his death.' Archbishop Welby added 'Crowther did not make himself grand. He lived out the commands of the words of his consecration. And from his time forwards God has demonstrated his grace through that ministry. Today, well over 70 million Christians in Nigeria are his spiritual heirs. Today, we honour him and in so doing The Lord Jesus Christ, whom he served. We are sorry for his suffering at the hands of Anglicans in this country. Learning from their foolishness and from his heroism, we seek to be a church that does not again exclude those whom God is calling. We seek new apostles and the grace to recognise them when they come'.

Soon after he resigned from active missionary work, and still having his faith in the Lord, Adjai wrote this:

'Looking back on my many and eventful years, I see abundant reason for thankfulness to the Giver of every good and perfect gift, and to say from my heart, 'Hitherto hath the Lord helped me.' He has graciously kept me from the hour when as a little slave boy, I was providentially saved from a life of misery and ignorance of Himself, and brought into contact with the Christian faith, through the instrumentality of the British Government and the Christian and persevering labour of the Church

Missionary Society, in faithful obedience to the comment of our ascended Lord 'Go and teach all nations.

If through my imperfect labour the work of God had been advanced on the Niger, the praise be ascribed to Him and not to me. I cannot expect to labour many years more in the cause of Christ, which lies so near to my heart, but it is my fervent prayer that these pages may be the means of leading others to enter the harvest field of Africa.'

When he resigned as Bishop from the Anglican Church, he went to live in Lagos with his daughter Abigail, and her husband the Rev. T. B. Macauley the founder and principal of Kings College, Lagos, the parents of Herbert Macauley, the veteran Nigerian politician. Here, I should mention that throughout his life Adjai was supported in his work by his devoted wife Asano, and his three daughters who were all married clergymen. This can be seen in this letter which was published in the Church Missionary Juvenile Instructor in 1865, from his daughter Julia Thomson, married to the Rev. Charles Thompson. The letter is dated 9 June, 1865 and was written in Lagos to thank a Miss Lanfear in Reading England:

'Dear Miss Lanfear,

I promised in my last to give you a longer account of the Niger Mission by this mail. My father has been in Sierra Leone to seek for Christian teachers, both for the Niger and Bonny stations. Those for Bonny he brought away with him to their stations, where they are now pretty comfortable settled - a schoolmaster and his assistant. King Peppel had promised to go halves in the share of establishing a Mission station in his country. With this my father has built a school large enough to contain seventy-five children, which is their present number. Forty-five of them have been examined by the bishop and found able to say the alphabet correctly. They are now learning to spell words of two and three letters.

You will be pleased to know that the books, slates and pencils from Reading are all they have had for use, so you can fancy how acceptable each present to the Niger Mission will continued to be. A box from another part of England supplied the school with needles, thread and thimbles. The bag from Reading, and the parcel from the two little girls are to go up further - to Onitsha, Igara, Idda and the Confluence; so, as it happens, we have not too many things yet, but I hardly like to intrude on your kindness. The jockey-cap sent in the last box is intended for a king: my sister Mrs Macaulay, is now covering it with beads and lace to make it look more fantastic. The red coats are all packed up to go by the 'Baylay'. My father will best know how to dispose of them when he writes you and Mrs. Malaher, which he considers as justly due. I hope, when we get up the Niger to take the entire charge of a girl's school. I shall from time to time call on Reading for bags, small clothes, needled and pins, and to coax my poor benighted little friends to come to school. You cannot fancy, dear friend, the amount of good effect a little red bag can produce, or a little skirt or jacket; what tears they will delight from not wanting to come to school.

Old dresses can sometimes be very useful for old women who cannot afford to buy them. I could give out every old frock, skirt, jacket to our old people who make coverings of themselves, and we have many aged people who come to church. I gave a skirt the other day to an old woman and begged her particularly not to wear it out of doors, as it was too shabby to give to anybody. But, what was my astonishment, three days after, to see the old lady coming with as many patches as there were holes in that skirt. I turned round quite amused and said, 'Nanny, why do you wear these clothes outside?' and she answered 'Missus, me old, and if me wear these clothes, no one will catch me.' On further examination, I found she had spent three days patching up the 'good, good clothes' as she calls them. I have no more such to give away, and there are any more who would be glad of them.

You will be sorry that the blockade has been placed on Abeokuta: the people feel it, but the Governor will not give way till they submit. The road to Ibadan continues open. May the Lord do what seemeth good in his time. I shall leave Lagos with reluctance, and my friends here, who often give me presents of parched corn and kola-nuts and salute me whenever we meet. With much desire for your warmest prayers on my new attempt,

I remain, dear Miss Lanfear,
Very truly your's,
Julia Thompson.'

His beloved wife of fifty years Asano, died on 19 October, 1880, a year after they had celebrated their Golden wedding anniversary. She took ill soon afterwards, and while her husband was away on his six monthly visits in the *Henry Venn* to the upper Niger. On his return he found his beloved wife and helpmate of fifty years near deaths door. Adjai in a letter to a friend later expressed his feelings, *'It was one of her earnest wishes during her long illness, that she might die in my arms, and this was granted her, though she never knew it, for she lay unconscious till her death. Though I am surrounded by a large family of children and grandchildren, yet the gap made by the absence of a fellow-companion for upwards of fifty years cannot easily be filled up- but we shall one day 'meet to part no more.'*

And to this, his old friend and mentor, the Rev. J. F. Schon also died. He had been like a father to Adjai and one to whom he could turn to for advice. His death was a great blow to Adjai in his advanced age.

Even though he had retired from the day to day politics of the church, yet he accepted invitations to peach and conduct services in various churches in the city. My grandmother told me that the last time she visited him, he was looking forward to making a trip to Bonny to preach at a confirmation ceremony. He also mentioned to her that he was disappointed that only one of his sons Dandeson, followed him into the church. He would have liked his other two sons, Josiah and Samuel to do the same but they followed the trade and commerce path and as none of his sons had children, he was also sad the Crowther name would die with him. But, that was not to be. For two of his daughters added 'Crowther' to that of their husbands names, so that the Crowther-Nicols' and the Crowther-Markes' still carry the name. In fact, there is a teenager living with his parents in Australia called Samuel Crowther-Marke and his brother is also named Adjai. One of the Grandsons of Adjai and my grandmother's brother Gurney, did become a priest. He was educated at Monkton Combe, Bath, under the Reverend Pocock, who was his guardian, then at Sidney College, Bath. He was admitted as a pensioner at Corpus Chriti College, Cambridge on 4 October,1875. He received his BA in 1879, and ordained a priest in 1883. His first appointment was at Holy Trinity Church, Freetown, and was later sent to a church in Bonthe in the south of Sierra Leone. But, as grandmother told me, he was not a robust person and he died in 1880, the same year as Asano, his grandmother. My grandmother also told me that she had made up her mind that if she had not been married by the time she reached thirty, she was going to train as a Deaconess and go and work with her uncle Dandeson in Bonny. But, luckily for me, marriage put a stop to her worthy plans, otherwise I would not be alive today to write about her Grandpa Adjai.

Adjai had a stroke in September 1891 which affected his right arm and leg and severely handicapped his speech. But, he insisted that he would get better and to continue with his travels to visit his missions on the Niger. He was told to rest by his doctors who advised that perhaps a visit to his son Dandeson at Bonny would do the trick. It did do the trick and his health did improve. In a letter he wrote to a friend from Bonny, he said that if he continued to improve like this, he would soon be able to return to resume his work. But, from his writing one can see that his hands shook as he wrote, but being the fighter that he was, he kept up his journal until Christmas Day, 1891 by which time he had returned to Lagos. On that day, he insisted on going to Morning service at the Cathedral Christ Church, even though he had difficulty moving around the house. That was not going to stop him from attending a service on Christmas Day, something he had done all his life. He was helped to church by Herbert Macauley his grandson.

It was planned that he would return to Bonny in the New Year, but it was not to be. **Samuel Adjai Crowther died peacefully on New Year's Eve 1891 and had a well-attended funeral on January 1, 1892.** His daughter, Mrs Macaulay with whom he was staying, has left a detailed account of his last hours on this earth:

'He was up as usual on the morning of January 31, dressed, and went through the morning devotion as he did every day; then he had tea after seven o'clock. About eight o'clock, he sent to call me to read a letter to him. I took the letter and read it and said: 'Father, I have read this letter to you several times.' He said: 'I have read it too,' (This was the last letter he got from the Secretary to the CMS, Salisbury Square)

I then said: 'If you want any more letters read to you , father, call for Charles (a grandson of his); he will read them to you. 'I am going to be busy with your breakfast.' He smiled and I left him sitting at the table, with his Prayer Book and hymn-book and some papers. At about nine o'clock, or so, an old Christian woman, Emma Taiwo,called to see the Bishop. I told her she could go and have a chat with him; he is not busy and will be leaving in a day or two for Bonny. She went into the parlour and returned in haste, and told me his head was not properly on the sofa. I ran in just in time to take hold of him, to save him from dropping from the sofa, and I called 'Father! Father!' He answered me. I said 'What is the matter?' He made no reply, but when I asked if he was cold he nodded and said 'Yes'. I ran for some brandy and water, which he drank and sent for Dr. Baudle, as Dr. O. Johnson was away from home.

After the attack he did not speak much, but answered when spoken to. At two o'clock in the afternoon, the doctor said he should go into his bedroom as the wind was blowing cold. He walked to the room supported. I had not the least thought there was anything serious, although I kept all the time with him. The doctor was in and out constantly: his last visit was at seven o'clock. He took the medicine patiently, sittingup. I said something about his coughing; he said 'No pain.'

At midnight when I came in to give him his medicine, he sat up and said he hoped it was the last dose. He lay down, and as I covered him I

said, 'Good night, father,' he said 'Good night.'
Half an hour later I heard movements in his room
and saw father just laying down, and I jumped on
the bed, for I saw he was dying. 'Father! Father!'
I cried. He heaved a sigh, and all was over. He
passed away at a quarter to one in the morning.'
RIP

His funeral the following day 1 January, 1892 took place at his beloved Christ Church. The address was given by the Rev James Johnson in both English and Yoruba, and the large congregation included the Governor and ten European and native clergy-men. The pall bearers who carried his coffin, which was strewn with native flowers, included his two grand sons. The first part at the ceremony at the graveside was conducted by Rev E.Pearse and the second part by the Archdeacon Hamilton, who conducted the committal. Unfortunately his son Archdeacon Dandeson Crowther, was not able to be at his father's funeral as he was then at Bonny and could not reach Lagos in time. But, he later wrote and spoke very highly, personalty and sympathetically about his father, throwing some light into the character of the Bishop not only as a public person, but as a father and husband.

At first he was buried at Ajele Cemetery in Lagos next to his wife and mother. This cemetery was then the most fashionable place for the great and the good of Lagos society to be incarcerated. Others who were buried there include Captain James Pinson Labulo Davies, the husband of Sally Forbes Bonetta, the adopted daughter of Queen Victoria, and Thomas Babington Macaulay, son-in-law of

Boshop Crowther and many other distinguished Lagos families. For over one hundred and fifty years, this cemetery was holy and sacred ground, but in 1971, the Lagos Government, under the then Governor, Brigadier Mobolaji Johnson, desired to use the site of the cemetery for new government offices. He issued notices to the families of the people buried there to remove the bodies. This act of evangelical vandalism was strongly opposed and condemned by the old established families in Lagos, and even by the Nigerian writer and poet Laureate Wole Soyinka, but to no avail. The then Anglican Bishop of Lagos, the Right Reverend Seth Kale, representing the families, delayed exhumation and reburial until 1976. Then an elaborate ceremony was held at a new burial site with a cenotaph within the compound of the Cathedral Christ Church, Marina, Lagos, next to his mother and beloved Asano, who had died twelve years earlier. There is a large East window dedicated to him in the Cathedral, and the name Crowther is commemorated in several churches and schools in Nigeria and Sierra Leone.

At the meeting of the Committee of the Church Missionary Society held in London, on the 2 January 1892, fulsome tribute was paid to Bishop Samuel Adjai Crowther, which was recorded in the minute's ledger.

'The committee received with much sorrow the tidings of the removal from the Church Militant of their revered friend the late Bishop Crowther. Few of Christ's Soldiers and servant have ever more remarkably from earliest years come into contact with the wickedness of this world, with the sad manifestation of human depravity, and few have more patiently carried on the battle against evil, and have maintained individually a more consistent course and a more unblemished reputation. This is by no means without the help of the Lord, with both intellectual vigour and moral character, Samuel Adjai Crowther is a conspicuous proof of the power of the Gospel, and the continued power of the Spirit of God in Christ's Church. Nothing else could have brought about with immense early disadvantage placed against his own judgement and the high position, surrounded by difficulties of almost unparalleled magnitude, often not receiving from the community, for reasons which cannot here be stated, that aid, counsel, cooperation and even encouragement, which he earned and solicited, he could yet have retained the respect and esteem of all who came contact with him, whether in his mission in Africa, or during his visits to this country; in this connection the Committee cannot but mention his unwearied industry, his absolute indifference to power, his considerations, his unflinching performance and all that he believed to be his duty, his unvaried kindliness towards all in thoughts and deed and the impression of nearness to the presence of God, which he uniformly produced on those who knew him. The Committee prays that those who remember him, especially in West African Christendom may be stirred to follow him in so far as he followed Christ and they offer their very sincere condolences to Archdeacon Crowther, to all the other relatives and friends of the late

Bishop and to the Christians of West African community.

On the death of Adjai, he was replaced by a European, which the CMS said was justified. Not until 1961, over sixty years after his death, when the West African Province was formed, that the second African bishop, the Rt. Rev. Moses Scott was consecrated and put in charge. Today there are many more bishops in the various Anglican dioceses all over West Africa, but Adjai was the first and only one for many years.

But, throughout his life Adjai never failed to be grateful to the Church Missionary Society for all it had done for him, from his early days when he first came under its wing.

When he died, the Church Missionary Society in London, in a rather tongue in cheek tribute to Adjai, placed on record these words. *'As regards the world, it is poorer for his removal. From his earliest years, in the providence of God, Samuel Crowther's lot was cast amidst some of the saddest manifestations of its wickedness and the depravity of the human heart; and in this environment he patiently and consistently carried on the battle against evil, maintaining throughout an unblemished reputation. As regards the church, he has most courageously fulfilled nearly thirty years, to the best of his abilities (and they were of no mean order), and with unremitting diligence and devotion, the duties of a Bishop under circumstances of almost unexampled difficulty and in face of very exceptional discouragements and disappointments. As regards* himself, *we may justly say that his life is a conspicuous proof of the power of the Gospel, and the continued presence of the Spirit of God in Christ's Church'.*

The Times of London carried his obituary on the 1 January, 1892. Headed BISHOP CROWTHER, it said: *'The Right Rev. BISHOP Crowther, first Bishop of the Niger Territory, terminated a long life of marked Christian simplicity and consistency on the last day of the year. A few weeks ago, according to information received by the Church Missionary Society, he had a slight paralytic seizure, but from the last letters, it did not appear that an early termination of life was expected.'*

I would like to end this memoire on the life of Adjai Samuel Crowther, my great-great-grandfather, by quoting from the inaugural lecture given by Jehu J. Hanciles, with his permission, at the opening of the Crowther Centre for Mission Education, CMS, Oxford, in 2008.

Throughout his adult life, Crowther had his full share of many critics and detractors, notably among Europeans who doubted his capability and questioned the advisability of promoting an African to positions of great visibility and responsibility. A longstanding criticism was that he had a timid character and was soft on discipline - a charge that overshadowed the last years of his life. And while he was widely venerated among African Christians (during his life and for long after), some African Christian leaders were concerned that circumstances made him a pawn in a high stakes game governed by European rules and expectations. But, Crowther's long life – he lived for almost all of the nineteenth century – and towering achievements defy straightforward analysis. He remains a complex figure who lived in a time of great transitions and shifting trends. For all his considerable indebtedness to European philanthropy and ideas, Crowther did much to undermine European missionary control mechanisms and lay the foundation for key elements of African Christianity. Bishop Adjai Crowther was not only the premier pioneer missionary of his day, he was also the most celebrated African Christian of the nineteenth century and one of the leading architects of the modern African Church.

ADJAI RESTS

THE END

DESCENDANTS OF BISHOP SAMUEL ADJAI CROWTHER

Generation No.1

1   BISHOP SAMUEL ADJAI CROWTHER born 1809* in Oshogun, Nigeria and died in 1891 in Lagos, Nigeria. He married SUSAN ASANO THOMPSON. She was born in 1815* and died in Lagos in 1888

Generation No. 2

2   Child of BISHOP SAMUEL ADJAI CROWTHER and SUSAN ASANO CROWTHER (nee THOMPSON) SUSAN CROWTHER born Freetown 1833 died Freetown in 1874. She married GEORGE POMPEY NICOL. He was born in Regent in 1833 and died in Freetown in 1909.

Generation No. 3

Child of SUSAN CROWTHER and GEORGE POMPEY NICOL , EMILIE KATHERINE CROWTHER-NICOL. Born in Freetown in 1866 and died in Freetown in 1965. Married GEORGE BRIGAS AWOONOR-WILLIAMS. He was born in Keta, Ghana in 1868 and died in Freetown in 1945.

Generation No. 4

3   Child of EMILIE KATHERINE CROWTHER-NICOL and GEORGE BRIGAS AWOONOR-WILLIAMS . VERA FRANCESS SISSY AWOONOR-WILLIAMS, was born in KETA,GHANA in 1902 and died in Freetown in 1984. She married RICHARD ONESIMUS GORDON, who was born in Gloucester in 1904 and died in Freetown in 1978.

Generation No. 5

4   Children of VERA FRANCESS SISSY AWOONOR-WILLIAMS, and RICHARD ONESIMUS GORDON

    i.   FRANCIS AWOONOR-GORDON born in Freetown in 1923 and died in Freetown 1999

    ii.   DOROTHY OMODELE MURIEL AWOONOR-GORDON. Born in Freetown in 1928, died in Freetown 1993. Married CHARLES THEOPHELUS BOISY PYNE born in 1926 in Freetown, died in Freetown 1991.

    iii. WILLIAM RICHARD AWOONOR-GORDON, born 1930 in Freetown and died in Freetown in 1977. Married YVETTE GUSSIE SPENCER-AUBER, born 1927

    iv. ARNOLD JEREMIAH AWOONOR-GORDON, born Freetown in 1933 (Author)

ADDENDUM

The number of books and booklets printed since Adjai's primer in 1849 was between eight hundred and one thousand. This represented one of the largest printed vernacular literature's in any African language. This is thanks to the successes of men like Adjai, Townsend, Gollmer and the many others who came after them, who between them had worked out many of the adequate solutions to translations. Between 1857 and 1893, over fifty such books and booklets were published in the languages of the lower Niger-Benue, and almost all were produced by West Africans, and all were due to the activities of the Niger Mission under Adjai. Here are some Adjai translated on his own or jointly with others.

1843 Samuel Crowther, Vocabulary of the Yoruba language. Part 1.

English and Yoruba. Part 11 – Yoruba and English. To which are prefixed, the grammatical elements of the Yoruba language. Published by C.M.S. London.

1849/52/3 S. Crowther The Yoruba Primer. Iwe ekinni. On ni fu awon ara Egba ati awon ara Yoruba. Published by C.M.S. London.

1850 S.Crowther. The Epistle of Paul the Apostle to the Romans. Translated into Yoruba for the use of the native Christians of that nation. Published by C.M.S. London. Printed at the expense of The B.F.B.S. in 500 copies.

1850-62 S.Crowther. Iwe adua Yoruba. A selection of from the Book of Common Prayer, translated into Yoruba according for the use of The native Christians of that nation. Published by the C.M.S. London.

1851 S. Crowther. The Gospel according to St. Luke, The Acts of the Apostles with the Epistles of St.James and St. Peters. C.M.S. London, printed at the expense of B.F.B.S.

1852 S.Crowther. A vocabulary of the Yoruba language, compiled by Crowther, together with introductory remarks by the Rev O.E.Vidal, M.A. Bishop designate of Sierra Leone.Published by Seeley, London.

1853 S. Crowther. The First Book of Moses, commonly called Genesis, translated into Yoruba and published by B.F.B.S. London

1854 S.Crowther. Second Book of Moses, commonly called Eksodus, translated into Yoruba, published by B.F.B.S. London

1854 S.Crowther. The Pslams of David translated into Yoruba, and published by B,F.B.S. London.

1856 S.Crowther. Iwe owe, ati iwe oniwasu. Li ede Yoruba, fu awon Kristian ti ilu nan, nipa Rev.S.C. alufa ti ilu nan.London: a ti ko fu awon egbe

Bibleti ti a npe ni Britise on ilu ni London. Printed for B.F.B.S.

1856 S.Crowther. Ihin rere ti S.Luke; ati ise awon apostolic; ati episteli to St. Paulu apostolic si awon ara Romu; pelu awon episteli St. Yakobu on St.Peteru. B.F.B.S. Londin

1857 Samuel Crowther, Isoama-Ibo primer, by Rev. S.C, native missionary of the C.M.S. Published by C.M.S. London.

1860 Samuel Crowther, Nupe Primer, published by C.M.S. London.

1860 S.Crowther, The first seven chapters of the Gospel according to St. Matthew in Nupe translated by Re. S.Crowther, published by British & Foreign Bible Society (B.F.B.S) London.

1861 S.Crowther and J.C.Taylor, Isuama-Ibo primer, revised and enlarged by Rev. J.C.Taylor. London.

1862 S. Crowther and T. King, The Epistles of St. Paul to the Phillippians, Colossians, Thessalonians, Timothy, Titus, Philemon and the Hebrews; the General Epistles of St. Jude; the General Epistles of St. John and the Revelation of St. John, translated into Yoruba by B.F.B.S, London.

1864 S.Crowther, A grammar and vocabulary of the Nupe language, compiled by the

Righ Rev. Samuel Crowther. D.D. Bishop of the Niger Territory. Published by C.M.S., London.

1877 S.Crowther, Labari wangi yan Yohanu, The Gospel according to St. John. Translated into Nupe by the Right. Rev.S.C., D.D., Bishop of the Niger Territory. Published by C.M.S., London.

1879 S.Crowther, Iwe adura Yoruba, ati ti ise-iranse awon sacramenti, ti o si ni liana mi ati isin-ilana, pelu awon Psalmu ti Dafidi, published byS.P.C.K. London

1882 S.Crowther, Vocabulary of the Ibo language, by the Right Rev.Bishop C. Published by S.P.C.K., London.

1883 S.Crowther & J.F. Schon, vocabulary of the Ibo language by the Right Rev. Bishop

REFERENCES

The main books and phamplets I consulted are:

From Slave Boy to Bishop. The story of Samuel Adjai Crowther.John Milstome, published by Lutterworth Press.

In the Shadow of the Elephant. Bishop Crowther and the African Missionary Movement. Inaugural Lecture by Jehu .Hanciles at the opening of the Crowther Centre for Mission Education, CMS, Oxford.

SAMUEL CROWTHER. The Slave Boy Who Became Bishop of the Niger, by Jesse Page, published by Forgotten Books.

THE EARLY STUDY OF NIGERIAN LANGUAGES: ESSAYS AND BIBLIOGRAPHIES By P.E.H. Hair, published by Cambridge at the University Press, in association with THE WEST AFRICAN LANGUAGES SURVEY AND THE INSTITUTE OF AFRICAN STUDIES, IBADAN.

Journal of an Expedition up the Niger and Tshadda Rivers, undertaken by Macgregor Laird, Esq. in connection with the British Government. By the Rev. Samuel Crowther. With map and appendix. British Library, Historical Print Editions, British Library.

Good Out of Evil, or the History of Adjai, by a Lady (a.f. Childe) with an Intr. Notice by C.F.Childe. A.F.Childe. Published by General Books.

Bishop Samuel Crowther c.1809-1891. The life of a humble man, Essay by Leslie Smith. 1998

A Charge delivered on the Banks of the River Niger in West Africa. Samuel Crowther. Published by Bibliolife

African Christianity by Adrien Hastings. A Geoffrey Chapman book, published by Cassell & Collier, Macmillian Publishers Limited.

The Inheritors, by Cameron W. Wilson, DYM Publishing.

The World Missionary Conference, Edinburgh 1910. Brian Stanley, published by William B. Eerdmans Publishing Company, Grand Rapids, Michigan/Cambridge UK.

The Church Missionary Society and World Christianity, 1799-1999. Edited by Kevin Ward and Brian Stanley and published by the Curzon Press.

Church Missionary Juvenile Illustrator. New Series Vol.111, i882. Published by the Church Missionary Society.

At Her Majesty's Request..An African Princess in Victorian England, by Walter Dean Myers.

The Black Bishop. Samuel Adjai Crowther, by Jesse Page, published by Hodder & Stoughton in 1908

Black and British, A forgotten History, by David Olusoga, published by Macmillan

A Patriot to the Core, Bishop Adjai Crowther, by J.E. Ajayi, published Spectrum Books

I thank them all for allowing me to read and make use of some of their materials they have written about Adjai Samuel Crowther.

Printed in Great Britain
by Amazon